500 Tips for Tutors

This book contains over 500 practical suggestions designed to help tutors establish active learning among their students. Divided into useful sections, the tips cover the gamut of teaching and learning situations and comprise a 'start anywhere', dip-in resource suitable for both the newcomer and the old hand.

Intended mainly for the university or college lecturer involved in learner-centred learning, the book offers fresh ideas and food for thought on six broad areas of the job:

- Getting your students going

- Starting off, and working together

- The programme itself – lectures, assignments and feedback

- Helping students to learn from resources

- Assessment: demonstrating evidence of achievement

- Skills for career and life in general

This lively and stimulating book will prove valuable to lecturers, tutors, teachers, trainers and staff developers.

Phil Race currently works part-time at the University of Leeds, and also runs training workshops for staff.

Sally Brown is Visiting Professor of Learning and Teaching at the Leeds Metropolitan University, and also at the Robert Gordon University in Aberdeen and Buckinghamshire Chilterns University College. She is also an independent higher education consultant, change manager and interim manager.

New editions in the 500 Tips series

500 Tips for Open and Online Learning, 2nd edition
Phil Race

500 Tips for Tutors, 2nd edition
Phil Race and Sally Brown

500 Tips on Assessment, 2nd edition
Phil Race, Sally Brown and Brenda Smith

500 Tips for Tutors
Second edition

Phil Race and Sally Brown

RoutledgeFalmer
Taylor & Francis Group

LONDON AND NEW YORK

First edition published 1993 by Kogan Page

Second edition published 2005 by RoutledgeFalmer
2 Park Square, Milton Park, Abingdon, Oxon, OX14 4RN

Simultaneously published in the USA and Canada
by RoutledgeFalmer
270 Madison Avenue, New York, NY 100016

RoutledgeFalmer is an imprint of the Taylor & Francis Group

© 1993, 2005 Phil Race and Sally Brown

Typeset in Garamond by Keystroke, Jacaranda Lodge, Wolverhampton
Printed and bound in Great Britain by MPG Books Ltd, Bodmin

British Library Cataloguing in Publication Data
A catalogue record for this book is available from the British Library

Library of Congress Cataloging in Publication Data
Race, Philip.
   500 tips for tutors / Phil Race and Sally Brown.— 2nd ed.
      p. cm. — (500 tips series)
   Includes bibliographical references and index.
   ISBN 0–415–34278–3 (pbk. : alk. paper)
      1. College teaching–Handbooks, manuals, etc. 2. Study skills–Handbooks, manuals,
etc. 3. Tutors and tutoring–Handbooks, manuals, etc. I. Title: Five hundred tips for
tutors. II. Brown, Sally, 1950 Feb. 1- III. Title. IV. Series.
   LB2331.R27 2004
   378.1′2—dc22   2004007610

ISBN 0–415–34277–5

Contents

Preface to the second edition

Little did we guess when in 1992 we were writing the original edition of *500 Tips for Tutors* that this was to be the first of over 20 'Tips' books we would write together, or separately, or with a range of co-authors. Our aim, then as now, was to provide practical advice for tutors and lecturers, based on experience, underpinned by the relevant scholarship of teaching and learning, but *about* practice rather than scholarship.

In the years since 1992, we have revisited teaching, lecturing, assessment, and many other things touched on in our original *500 Tips for Tutors*, and have written on all of these in much more depth and detail in other works. So we returned with not a little trepidation to the task of making a new edition of the first of our joint books. Having between us written *2000 Tips for Lecturers, 500 Tips on Assessment, Lecturing: A Practical Guide* and *The Lecturer's Toolkit*, did we have anything new to say, and how on earth could we cover the ground in just 500 Tips now?

Fortunately, when we returned to the agenda of *500 Tips for Tutors*, we were reminded of two things. The book was for 'tutors' and not just lecturers – in other words, for *all* the people supporting students rather than just those designing teaching and assessment. So, as well as being relevant to lecturers, the book needed to continue to be appropriate for teaching assistants, postgraduate students with teaching responsibilities, and other staff supporting student learning in educational institutions. Furthermore, the book was essentially about 'helping students to learn' – supporting them in many different aspects of their experience in higher and further education. Meanwhile, Phil had written several study-skills books directly for students. Yet in most of our subsequent joint books we'd concentrated on teachers, so here now was our opportunity to go back to the vital agenda of helping teachers to help students to learn effectively.

So how best could we go about the task of putting our shared experience into this new edition? It now would be quite impossible to cram all our ideas on helping colleagues to help students to learn into just 500 Tips. So we decided to work mainly with the agendas in the original book, and update and deepen them in the light of our current experience and thinking.

In practice, this has meant that just about every tip from the original volume has been changed, expanded, refined, deepened and polished, yet the original agenda has been broadly retained. Our new edition aims to continue to achieve the outcome of helping you to help your students to have a successful educational experience.

Phil Race and Sally Brown
March 2004

Chapter 1

Getting your students going

In this section, we start by looking at ways in which your students can be helped to do some useful preparation before they start your programme, then suggest how you can help them explore their own learning strategies. Then we remind you of a selection of general study skills that can be useful to students throughout their studies, or on particular occasions.

1

Helping students to prepare to start learning

Before the start of a programme or module, there may be a vacation or other slack time when students could, if they wished, do much to pave their way towards success. To be able to do so, they need to know what might be useful things for them to do to prepare for your programme. Here are some ways to help them.

1   **Make sure they're given appropriate information.** For example, try to ensure that students are given printed documentation about your programme (or your part of a course) some time in advance. A syllabus, for example, can be a useful start – better still, a programme or module handbook. If you know they've all got appropriate access, such material can be useful online.

2   **Get them pre-reading.** Give them a list providing some ideas about useful sources to consult before the programme begins. The shorter and more focused such a list is, the more likely it is that students will try to do some pre-reading.

3   **Tell them why.** Explain why it's useful to study each major piece, and give positive suggestions regarding what students should try to extract from each source. Arming students with lists of questions can be a very productive way of helping them focus their reading. Build in tasks to accompany their pre-reading, including specific short tasks, such as 'from Chapter 3 of Smith and Jones work out the three most important questions to ask about Bloggs's theory'.

4   **Alert students to the intended learning outcomes.** The sooner they know about the standards they will eventually need to achieve, the more they can adjust their expectations about your programme. Giving examples of aims, learning outcomes, relevant assessment criteria and last year's exam questions can be useful ways of helping students to tune in to the level of your programme.

5   **Consider giving them a pre-learning package.** Although this may take some time for you to put together, it can serve a valuable role in years to come. It can help to provide you with an identified starting level for the whole group. A useful package will be a mixture of information, references, tasks and activities, with particular attention being given to designing printed *responses* to the tasks and activities, so that students working alone through the pre-course package have the benefit of feedback on their attempts.

6   **Give them a pre-programme checklist.** For example, provide students with a list of 'useful things to do before starting this programme'. Some of these things could involve brushing up on relevant past learning. Other elements could include ideas and thoughts to collect together, and perhaps suggestions for a little preliminary experimentation or fieldwork.

7   **Advise them on what to bring to the first sessions on the programme.** Such advice is always welcomed by students. However, they need something better than a list of the recommended reading. They need a 'user-friendly' guide to what will be really useful in the first days of the programme. It can be useful to enlist the help of some students who have finished the programme (successfully) to put together a 'what to get beforehand' check-list.

8   **Get last year's students to help this year's students to find their feet.** Try getting past students to draft a letter to new students, which can be a valuable way of breaking the ice with the new students. This is particularly relevant when your contribution is at the very start of an entire programme. Such letters can be accompanied by up-to-date information – for example, the times and places of the first few components of your part of their programme.

9   **It's never too early to point students towards the study skills they will need to develop.** It can be useful to recommend one or two useful sources of study skills advice that are directly relevant to your programme or module (or better still, write some key suggestions yourself).

10 **Don't send too much information!** When sending out ideas for pre-programme preparation, ensure that students won't feel snowed under by a mass of paperwork. If it all looks too daunting, they'll probably do none of it – and maybe they won't arrive at all. A 'front sheet' summarising the bits and pieces in your 'pre-programme' pack – and with several marked 'optional' – can help students take a balanced view of it all.

2

Helping students to explore how they learn best

The more students know about the processes by which they learn best, the more they can harness those processes to their advantage. It is useful to build in some study-skills discussion right at the beginning of your programme, alongside the first bits of learning. Students will then see that you're interested in helping them find out not only *what* to learn, but also *how best* to go about it. The following ideas can be used to help students take ownership of some key steps in the ways they learn.

1   **Start with their achievements.** Ask your students to think of something they're good at, and to jot it down.

2   **Get them thinking about *how* they have already achieved things.** For example, ask them to write down a few words explaining *how* they became good at whatever it was.

3   **Get them reflecting on how they learned things well.** Help them compare their responses to the previous two questions. For example, most students will have used words such as 'doing it', 'practice', 'repetition', 'trial and error', 'getting it wrong at first'. Use these ideas to help them see that most learning is done in an active way. Remind them how useful it can be to learn by making mistakes, and how therefore it is useful to regard mistakes as valuable learning experiences.

4   **Help them see that 'learning' is down to them.** We can't do it for them! Comment on how rarely people declare that they became good at something simply by 'being taught' or 'being shown how', and so on. From this, draw out the need for students to take an active part in the various teaching–learning situations they encounter, rather than sitting passively 'being taught and hoping it will stick'.

5   **Ask students to think of something they *feel* good about.** Ask them (for example) to identify a personal attribute or quality about which they feel a sense of pride, and then to jot it down. Next, ask them to write down a few words explaining *upon what basis* they feel good about whatever they wrote down in answer to the previous question. In other words, ask them, 'Upon what evidence do you have this positive feeling?'

6   **Help students to realise how important feedback can be.** By far the most frequent answers to 'how do you know you feel good about this?' include phrases such as 'other people's reactions', 'feedback from other people', 'the expressions on people's faces', 'people come back to me for help', and so on. In other words, the keys to positive feelings tend to be feedback, and other people. This can be a useful way of helping students develop a healthy 'thirst for feedback' rather than trying to hide from situations where other people see how they're doing.

7   **Remind students that studying is not a completely separate part of their lives.** The same processes that lead to becoming good at anything in life also apply to successful studying. Similarly, the same processes that lead to positive feelings about anything in life also apply to developing positive feelings about studying.

8   **Help students to learn from disasters as well as triumphs.** Ask them to think of some learning experience that went wrong, and to write down a few words about what happened to make it an unsuccessful learning experience.

9   **Help them to compare the causes of poor learning experiences.** Common causes relate to a lack of feedback (therefore lack of positive feelings) and to lack of opportunity to practise (therefore a lack of 'learning by doing'). Other causes are lack of motivation – in other words, no deep wish to succeed – or a lack of time to make sense of it all, or no time to reflect.

10   **Highlight for your students the main factors underpinning successful (and enjoyable) learning.** These are:

- wanting to learn – a sense of purpose;
- needing to learn – being clear about their targets and the standards to aim for, knowing why things are important;
- learning by doing – practice, experimentation, repetition, trial and error;
- feedback – from each other, from tutors, from handouts, from Web sources, all leading to positive feeling about what has been learned;

- making sense of what has been learned – getting their heads round it, 'digesting' it, putting it into perspective.

It can be useful to keep reminding students of the importance of all these factors as they continue into your programme, and helping them work out ways of taking ownership of the importance of these factors as they develop their learning processes in the context of the content of your programme.

3

Helping students to develop time-management skills

The same number of hours in each day is given to everyone, but time-management skills are widely underdeveloped. If we can manage our time well, we can manage just about everything else. The ten suggestions that follow can help students increase their mastery over time.

1   **Help students to see what's in it for them to become better at time management.** Help them to work out the benefits of well-developed time-management skills. Help them to see that personal productivity, personal efficiency and personal effectiveness are all connected to their ability to manage time. Allow them to work out that time-management skills have lifelong value and enhance all their other skills and aptitudes – and in due course enhance their employability too.

2   **Get students thinking consciously about learning pay-off.** Ask them what kinds of activity have a high pay-off in terms of learning. These can include discussing, explaining, summarising, problem-solving and quizzing each other. Ask them what kinds of activity have low learning pay-off; these can include writing in copying mode, reading passively, and appearing to listen. Time is too precious to squander on actions that have only low learning pay-off.

3   **Help students to stop and look back.** Get them to reflect on things they have learned, rather than simply hope that the learning has happened by magic. Ask them to work out *how* their learning happened, exactly *what* they learned, exactly *when* the learning happened, and how it can be made more efficient next time.

4   **Help students to spare themselves from the effects of procrastination.** Show them how wasteful and miserable just *thinking* about work can be – compared with simply getting on with it. Time spent thinking about work has associations with a guilty conscience, and looming tasks. Time

7

spent *after* work has been successfully completed is high-quality time – the most enjoyable sort of time. But recognise that this is a counsel of perfection, which we ourselves don't always abide by!

5   **Encourage students to get stuck in straight away.** Remind them how often 90 per cent of things tend to get done in the last 10 per cent of the time available. Point out that it is therefore logical that most things can be done in the *first* 10 per cent of the time available – leading to the luxury of having much more genuinely 'free' time. Hint at the positive feelings and confidence that come with always having things done well ahead of schedule – and indeed the security of knowing that there is room to accommodate the odd unexpected hiccup or crisis.

6   **Get students to set stage deadlines for themselves.** Encourage them to set several stage deadlines rather than one final deadline. Encourage them to break large tasks into manageable chunks. Encourage them to set dead-lines 'early' to allow for the unexpected.

7   **Help students feel positive about getting ahead of schedule.** Point out the benefit of doing half an hour's work on a non-urgent task each time before starting an urgent one. The urgent one will still get done, as there is pressure to complete it. The practice of doing a little non-urgent work gradually leads to a situation in which there are fewer and fewer urgent tasks. Point out that human nature is such that 'urgent' is often synonymous with 'late', but that this situation can be countered by conscious adjustment of study patterns.

8   **Get students to do a risk assessment.** Help them to identify the con-sequences for them of poor time management. Help them to see where their own particular risks lie. When they are aware of the risks and the conse-quences, they are much more likely to adjust their study habits to compensate for these.

9   **Help students to maximise their use of peer support.** Get them to use each other in setting and monitoring deadlines. Show them that the more people know about a deadline, the more likely it is to be met.

10 **Convince students that minutes can count for more than hours.** Few people have many free two-hour windows in their week; everyone has lots of five-minute windows. Using just some of the short time slots for study-related tasks can pay much higher dividends than putting everything off until a two-hour window comes along.

4

Helping students to develop task-management skills

Task management is at least as important as time management. The following suggestions can help your students to sort out the respective priorities of the various tasks that they need to carry out in the course of their studies.

1   **Explain how useful 'to do' lists can be.** It's much more efficient than trying to carry round in one's mind all that needs to be done.

2   **Get students to prioritise their tasks.** Five categories can be useful: 'must be done today', 'should be done today', 'may be done today', 'could be started today', 'not necessary today'. This can be done, for example, using Post-it™ notes for the tasks, and a wallchart. Items can be moved up the wall as they become more urgent. Point out the value of choosing tasks from more than one category on each day. In other words, just doing 'must be done today' tasks does not help to prevent a backlog building up, whereas doing (or starting) one or two low-priority tasks each day has the long-term benefit of preventing an accumulation of urgent tasks.

3   Suggest that students make an **'urgency/importance' grid,** and decide which tasks go in which box.

Urgent but not important	Urgent and important
Neither urgent nor important	Important but not urgent

Then suggest the following strategy:

A Do one 'important but not urgent' task first.

B Then get on with an 'urgent and important' task, but without spending *too much* time or energy on it.

C From time to time, do an 'urgent but not important' task as a relaxation from doing important tasks.

D Try to drop or delegate 'neither urgent nor important' tasks, or occasionally do one of them as relaxation from everything else.

4 **Remind students that a task is often done more easily if it is not really urgent.** When something must be completed at once, it tends not to be approached in a relaxed and creative way, and is therefore rarely done really well.

5 **Encourage at least some multi-tasking.** Suggest that it may be better to do three things on the list today (even without finishing any of them) rather than to spend all the available time on one task.

6 **Suggest investing in a rewards strategy.** Encourage students to allocate themselves rewards on the completion of tasks (or major stages in a big task) – and encourage them to be appropriately creative in their definitions of 'rewards'.

7 **Remind students of people power!** Explain the usefulness of letting other people know about one's plans. If friends or family are likely to come up to one and ask, 'Did you get that task done you were telling me about?', there is a considerable incentive not to be 'caught lacking'. Let your students know of one of your own projected deadlines for a task.

8 **Help students to celebrate tasks completed.** Few things give more satisfaction than ticking off from a list things that have been completed.

9 **Suggest that students use 'targets' as well as 'deadlines'.** A 'deadline' is likely to be imposed externally, whereas 'targets' can be chosen by themselves. The feeling of ownership of targets makes it highly attractive to try to meet them (especially when other people are aware of these targets).

10 **Lead by example.** Show students your own approaches to managing the various tasks in a typical day or week. Share approaches that are effective – but even better, share your approaches that fail! Learning from other people's mistakes is a particularly attractive way to learn.

5

Helping students to identify the questions they need to answer

'If you already know what the questions are, you're more than halfway towards being able to answer them' – how often have we told students this! However, they often seem to need some help before they make good use of question-devising strategies in their studies.

1   **Point out that students' learning is most often assessed in terms of their ability to answer questions.** Written exams usually test this, as do oral exams and interviews. Remind students that the ability to answer questions, like any other skill, is developed best by practice.

2   **Help students to identify *reasonable* questions.** Suggest that they continuously ask themselves, 'What may I reasonably be expected to be able to do with this?' Suggest that they pose this question to themselves during lectures, while reading, in tutorials, and in every part of their studies. The word 'reasonable' is important: there's no point in their trying to prepare for things that are not feasibly achievable (for example, learning massive amounts of numerical or statistical data).

3   **Encourage students to accumulate their thinking about such questions.** Encourage them to make themselves 'question banks'. Suggest that these should contain large numbers of short, sharp questions, based on what they think may be expected of them. Suggest that when they know how to answer a wide range of short, sharp questions, they will automatically be in a strong position to put together answers to longer, complex questions – for example, exam questions.

4   **Advise students to get hold of past exam papers.** Suggest they do this early in the programme (if they leave this till later, they may find them frightening and be thrown off their stride in their revision!). Suggest that they

break the exam questions down into shorter, sharper components, and add these to their question banks.

5   **Practice makes perfect.** Remind students that becoming able to do things depends mainly on practice. Therefore, it is of little value just *reading* through questions and answers. Point out that when an answer is in sight, their eyes will stray straight to it, which will rob them of any real chance to start practising with the question.

6   **Remind students that there should be no complete surprises.** Point out to them that case studies, worked examples, and problems that are shown to them in lectures and tutorials may well be very closely related to the things that they in turn will be expected to be able to do in exams. Therefore, suggest that they add the *questions* from things covered in class or independent study to their question banks.

7   **Point out that coursework is based on tasks and questions.** Advise them that things such as essays, assignments, tutorial exercises and practical-work questions can all be the basis of similar exam questions. Suggest that they add all such questions to the content of their question banks, and use them for practice.

8   **Two heads can think of more – and better – questions than one.** Encourage students to compile question banks collaboratively. A group of students will quickly build up a more comprehensive question bank than an individual.

9   **Questions come before answers.** Suggest to students that it's well worth writing down and storing questions even before they know the answers. If they have the question on file, sooner or later there will be a way of finding out the answer. If the question were not put on file, the question itself could quickly be forgotten.

10   **Variety is the spice of becoming able to answer questions.** Since practising answering questions is such valuable practice for exams, suggest that students do it in as many ways as they can: written answers, 'mental' answers and oral answers. Working in small groups is a particularly effective way of getting through a lot of question-answering in a short time, for example by students quizzing each other using a question bank.

6

Helping students to read more actively

The term 'reading for a degree' has been around for a long time, yet reading is a skill that relatively few students have developed as systematically as they can. The following suggestions may help students take more control of their reading styles.

1   **Remind students how easy it is to read passively.** In other words, just reading something often yields low learning pay-off. You could demonstrate this to them in a large-group session by giving them a handout with some printed information, then later in the session testing them on the content. Suggest that time spent 'just reading' can be almost wasted as far as real learning is concerned, and that they can and should develop additional ways of focusing their attention as they read.

2   **Point out the value of jotting down questions *before* reading something.** It then becomes 'reading with an agenda in mind' and is automatically more active. As answers to the questions are found, they tend to register.

3   **Help students to make good use of their sources and resources.** Remind them that the most important pages of textbooks are often the contents pages and the index. Suggest that tracking down the *relevant* information is one of the most important aspects of good reading skills, and information retrieval skills are just as useful with online sources as with textbooks and journal articles.

4   **Suggest that *active* reading is normally done with a pen!** For example, making summary notes and mental maps are useful ways of helping ensure that the important ideas are being distilled and refined during reading.

5   **Get students primed to make lists of questions as they read.** Any important information can simply be regarded as the answers to some questions. The measure of how effectively they have read something depends on how well they can identify the questions it addressed, and then

answer these questions on it. These questions can later serve as triggers for the important information they have been reading about, and can be used as summaries to aid revision.

6   **Give students suggestions about when speed-reading can be useful.** For example, when doing a preliminary 'skim' of a large body of information, speed-reading is very useful for creating a mental map of the information available. Suggest that students check that they are not 'stuck' in a 'recitation' mode of reading (often picked up at school in reading-aloud exercises), where the speed of reading is limited to the speed at which students can 'hear' the words in their minds. Help them to realise that they can read several times faster than they can 'hear'.

7   **Help students to identify how best to find out what a paragraph is about.** For some kinds of information, reading just the first sentence of every paragraph can be enough. This technique is particularly useful as part of a process of finding the most relevant paragraphs, which can then be read more slowly and thoroughly.

8   **Encourage students to personalise their source materials.** When they own their own books, recommend that they 'make their books their own' – for example, by writing on them, using highlighter pens, photocopying crucial extracts and arranging them in a scrapbook format, and so on. The same applies to handout materials, and printouts from material downloaded from the Web. (Obviously, advise against defacing library copies. Further-more, recognise that many students nowadays 'buy to sell back', so that annotating their books with Post-it™ notes can be the most suitable approach to personalising them temporarily.)

9   **Quality of reading counts more than quantity of reading.** Encourage students to be selective. Advise them that quality of reading and relevance are much more important than mere breadth of reading – especially when preparing for written exams. Only so much can be written in an exam room.

10 **Point out the danger of using reading as a work avoidance tactic!** Despite the various ways of improving the quality of reading, remind students that most 'high-pay-off learning' is learning by doing in one form or another – not just reading. Activities such as practising answering questions on what has been read have higher learning pay-off than does reading.

7

Helping students to get their heads round what they've learned

When you only have a given number of hours to cover your parts of a programme with students, it is all too easy to fill all the available hours with planned teaching. It is important to accommodate students' need for time to reflect on what they are learning, and to take stock of how their learning is going.

1   **Being there is only one part of the picture.** Keep reminding students that it is not enough for them simply to be there at lectures, tutorials, laboratory classes, and so on. In addition, they need to work out their own ways of consolidating what they are learning, doing coursework and preparing for assessment. They need to take on the responsibility for making sense of it all, and getting up to speed regarding being able to answer questions on it, solve problems with it, and so on.

2   **Get students processing what they've learned.** Devise short tasks to set students, such that they necessarily reflect on material they have been introduced to. Give the tasks out as (for example) structured task-sheets at the end of lectures, or post them online immediately after each lecture. Such tasks can be the basis of tutorial and seminar activities.

3   **Find out how students think their learning is going.** One way of allowing students to reflect on learning experiences is to ask them to provide you with feedback about their learning. Issuing a questionnaire asking (for example) them to categorise various topics into 'completely understand', 'more or less understand' and 'don't yet understand' gives you feedback about their progress, but also helps them to reflect on their individual positions (and to compare their feelings with colleagues').

4   **Play it again – and again if it's important.** Explain the importance of repetition in learning and understanding. Suggest that it's more useful to go

over something for a few minutes several times than to spend one long spell studying it. Explain that when they are repeatedly spending a short time studying something, their subconscious mind is continuing to process the information and make sense of it.

5   **Suggest useful reflection techniques to students.** For example, get them to review a lecture by deciding their answer to a question such as 'if there were just two things I would need to remember from this lecture, they would be (1) . . . and (2) . . . '

6   **Encourage students to find out what has actually happened in their minds.** Remind students of the dangers of reading passively – just turning the pages without any real learning occurring. Suggest that they stop and reflect at frequent intervals on what they have just been reading, for example by making a short summary or mind map of it, or by turning what they have learned into a list of short questions to quiz themselves with later.

7   **Build some reflection-type activities into your teaching sessions.** For example, use a lecture period now and then to pose to the class a series of problems or issues based on material they have met already, first getting students to reach individual decisions or answers, then initiating a discussion or debriefing with the whole group.

8   **Make sure that students will consolidate what they have covered.** For example, when deciding topics for student-led seminars, help to ensure that the preparation for the seminars will include reflecting on material that has already been covered in the programme, and linking it to the specific topics of the seminars. This helps students to see what we actually mean when we place emphasis on reflective learning.

9   **Reflection can happen just about anywhere.** Advise students that they can use all sorts of times and places to reflect. A considerable amount of reflection can be done in just a few minutes. Odd bits of time that might otherwise be completely wasted can be used for useful reflection – for example, waiting in a queue, train journeys, boring bits of lectures, and so on.

10 **Help students to realise how useful their classmates can be to them.** Enthuse students regarding how useful it can be to deliberately reflect with a few of their peers. Two or three people looking back at a lecture (or something they have all just read) can come up with more ideas than any one person would have, and because they are explaining their ideas by putting them into words to each other, the ideas will be more firmly registered in their minds, leading to deeper learning.

8

Organising your studies: a checklist for students

The set of questions that follows can be used as a discussion starter when you're working with a class or tutorial group, especially not too close to the time when they should be getting down to some systematic revision or consolidation. Most of the questions are 'trick' ones, in that if students have definite answers to them, it may be an indication of the existence of some 'study avoidance tactics'!

1 Have you already established a regular study schedule?

2 If not, do you think you should be making yourself a regular study schedule?

3 Where is the best place for you to study?

4 Do you find yourself wasting lots of time finding your bits and pieces before you actually get started on a spell of studying?

5 Is your desk or table cluttered when you start studying?

6 Are you doing enough reading?

7 When is the best time for you to do some studying?

8   At what times is your home environment most conducive to studying?

9   How long does it take you to do a useful element of studying?

10   What is the minimum time it is worth you using? (For example, 15 minutes comes up often even in a busy life, yet is long enough to do some useful study-related task.)

11   What do you do with odd bits of time – train journeys, waiting for people, waiting in queues, and so on?

12   Do you sit watching TV with a guilty conscience?

13   Are you worried about how much studying your classmates may be doing?

14   When you're studying, do you regularly stop and check that it is really 'going in'?

15   What are your three favourite 'studying avoidance tactics' and what can you do to overcome these?

16   What in-built interferences do you accept? (For example, can you study with the TV on in a corner, or working alongside chatty friends? Can you leave your mobile phone on in case someone rings you or texts you?)

17   Are you doing sufficient studying?

18   How can you tell whether or not you're doing sufficient studying?

Chapter 2

Starting off, and working together

In this section, we look at ways of getting to know your students, and ways of helping them to work together effectively in small groups. We also present some ideas about ways of helping students make best use of other people, including yourself.

9

Finding out what students already know

It has been said that for more than half the time that students spend in formal teaching–learning situations, they are listening to things they already know. The following suggestions can help overcome such a situation.

1 **Help students to value what they already know.** Suggest to them that their existing knowledge is really useful and is worth holding on to, consolidating and building upon.

2 **Find out what students can already do.** Give them a numbered list of questions and ask them to privately brainstorm which questions they can already answer. Find out by a show of hands how many in the group feel they can already answer each question in turn. Helping students to see that they already know the answers to at least some of the questions boosts their confidence, and helps you to see which questions to focus on as you continue to work with them.

3 **Try a visual alternative.** Try a 'public' brainstorm about what your students already know – and don't yet know. Put a short set of questions on one or more flip charts and ask students to go round putting ticks beside the questions they can definitely answer, crosses beside those they can't yet answer, and question marks beside those they are not sure they can answer.

4 **Conduct a group brainstorm.** Ask students in groups to list things they already know about particular topics, then allow members of different groups to explain particular things in more detail to other groups.

5 **Try a Post-it™ knowledge brainstorm.** For example, give each student a Post-it™ note and ask them to jot down on it the most important thing they already know about the sub-topic you're going to be working with them on next. Ask them to stick the Post-its™ onto a flip chart or wall, and celebrate

what the whole group already knows. Use this display as your agenda for what they need to find out about next.

6   **Try a Post-it™ question brainstorm.** Give out Post-it™ notes to the whole class. Ask everyone to write out questions they already know the answer to, and add their names to the Post-its™ before displaying them on a wall. Use the collected Post-its™ as the start of an agenda addressing both the knowledge students already have, and the gaps you identify in the total pattern of knowledge.

7   **Get them mind-mapping in groups.** Allocate different topics to different groups. Ask each group to prepare on a flip chart a mind map of things they already know about their topic. Ask groups to exhibit their flip charts and stand by them explaining their mind maps to students from other groups touring the exhibition.

8   **Get students learning by explaining what they already know to each other.** Ask each student to choose something he or she already knows, then explain it to the rest of the group. Probably the greatest benefit comes from finding the words to explain things, thereby consolidating understanding. People often learn more from the act of explaining things to others than from having things explained to them.

9   **Get students to identify questions they can already answer.** Ask everyone to think of something they already know, then turn it into a question to which their knowledge is the answer. Then ask students, in groups, to pose the questions to each other and take turns explaining their answers to each other.

10 **Devise pre-tests** to use to find out what your students already know, but not to 'test' them in a threatening way. Explain that the objective is to show them how much they already know and to let you see what you don't need to explain to them.

11 **Get students in groups to draft out answers to longer questions.** Early in the study programme, provide a selection of typical formal assignment questions (or typical examination questions) and ask groups of students to prepare *outline* answers to questions of their choice (taking far less time than writing out full answers). Discuss with the whole class the strengths of each outline answer and point out any important things that would need to be added to the outlines to lead to good full answers.

10

Helping students to make sense of the learning programme

Almost certainly, one of the first things you were given when you began to prepare to teach your first programme was documentation of one kind or another. This probably contained details of the intended learning outcomes – in other words, what students should be able to show for their learning when they have successfully completed their learning on that part of their studies. Strangely, despite the fact that such things are written to describe what is to be learned, such documents don't always find their way into the hands of students themselves. Here are some suggestions about how you can use the documentation to help structure students' learning activities.

1   **Check whether students have actually received the details.** Find out whether your students already have their own copies of programme documentation (for example, in a programme or departmental handbook), or whether they know where to find them online. If they do not, give them at least a copy of your own part of their programme, and if possible the rest as well.

2   **Translate the programme information into English!** (It might presently be written in 'academese'!) When students know what they are expected to be learning, they're in a better position to go about their task of learning it. It helps them if you translate their programme into intended learning outcomes in language that the students themselves can understand, so that they can see exactly what sort of things they are, in due course, going to be expected to achieve.

3   **Focus on evidence of achievement.** When you explain exactly what a particular learning outcome means in practice, it is helpful to describe the sort of evidence which indicates that it has been successfully achieved. This helps students to work out what the standards are.

4   **Explain why – build in the rationale.** Intended learning outcomes can be very useful for letting students know *what* they will be learning, but sometimes students also need some explanation regarding *why* they need to put energy into learning particular things. It is not always obvious to them why they have to learn things – and naturally, if they can't see a good *reason* for learning something, they're not going to invest much mental energy into trying to learn it.

5   **Explain how – clarify the processes.** Illuminate the 'learning map' even further by explaining to students which teaching and learning contexts will be used as they cover the various parts of their programme. For example, some things will be covered by lectures, others may be dealt with in seminars and tutorials, and yet other things may be delegated altogether to students to undertake by private reading, or group work, or using open learning packages.

6   **Explain the time dimensions.** Relevant documentation can provide a useful map of the content of a programme. The map is made much more useful by adding some details regarding the timescales involved. For example, it may take several weeks to 'crack' an important early part of a programme, while some later parts may be very straightforward thereafter. If students already know approximately how long each part is going to take, they have a better sense of which parts are likely to be most important.

7   **Explain which parts you will be covering in depth.** In any programme, it's unlikely that everything will be covered in an 'even' manner. Let students know which parts of the programme you'll be spotlighting and which parts you'll just be skimming over, or indeed leaving to the students to cover for themselves. Confirm with them the respective expectations regarding assessment – particularly reminding them about the assessment elements that will link to those parts you're not going to be spotlighting in class with them.

8   **Let students know when you go on a diversion.** There may be occasions when it is best for you (and for your students) to depart from the published programme. For example, when it is relevant to develop a topical theme to illustrate a fundamental principle, it may be useful to cover completely new ground with them. Let them know of such 'departures' – and particularly let them know which parts of the 'old' programme have now been replaced. Be careful, of course, to make sure that any forthcoming assessment takes into account the newly added areas.

9   **Design assessment with the intended learning outcomes firmly in sight and mind.** Towards the end of a programme, the published learning outcomes should provide students with a solid basis upon which to work out exactly what they should be able to do to provide *evidence* of their

achievement of the intended outcomes. For example, make sure that you write examination questions with the intended outcomes very much in mind, avoiding any possibility that students find completely unexpected questions that they could not reasonably have prepared for.

10   **Be honest with students if time runs out!** If this happens, alert students to any parts of the programme that are not going to be covered by your teaching – or by the associated assessment. Resist the temptation to cram the last few lectures full of all the remaining parts of the programme; if exams are coming up shortly, few students are going to spend much time on newly acquired information in any case.

11

Getting to know you

People in general tend to take more notice of people they know. Your students will take more notice of you if they feel that they know you – and, above all, that you know them. They will learn more from each other if they know each other better. Getting their names right is a useful step towards building up the sort of relationship that fosters learning. It is also useful to help students to get to know each other – not only in small-group contexts, but also in lecture contexts, which can actually be quite lonely for some students. The following suggestions link ways of getting to know names with some general 'icebreaker' tactics you may find useful.

1   **Remember that the use of names can be linked strongly to feelings.** Think how *you* feel when someone gets your name wrong – especially someone you would have expected to know it. One of the problems with large groups is that members of the group can feel quite anonymous and alone. Decide to tackle the situation.

2   **Find out their preferred names.** At the beginning of the programme, ask students 'What do you *want* to be called?' The names they give you will be more accurate than your printed class lists, and you'll quickly find out whether Aziz wants to be called Az, Patricia – Pat, and so on.

3   **Give students the chance to get to know each other's names.** At early stages it's useful to give students sticky labels to write their names on in bold felt-tip pen, then ask them to stick the labels to their clothing for the duration of a session. This gives *you* the chance to call them by the name they prefer – and gives them the chance to start getting to know each other. This can work in large lecture groups as well as small tutorial or seminar groups. Sticky labels are quite cheap!

4   **In relatively small-group contexts, try memory by association.** With 10 to 20 students, for example, try a round as follows: 'Tell us your name,

and tell us something *about* your name.' This can be a good icebreaker, and can be very memorable too, helping people develop association links with the names involved.

5   **Try going round in circles?** Another way of getting a small group of students to know each other is to get them sitting in a circle. Ask one to say his or her name, then the person to the left to say, 'I am . . . and this is my friend . . . ' Carry on round the circle, adding one name at each stage, till someone goes right round the circle correctly.

6   **Love and hate relationships?** A further way of getting to know students' names is to ask them to introduce themselves, stating first their names and then something they like and something they dislike. It's most effective when the subject matter is relatively uncontroversial, such as 'I like cats but I hate cheese.'

7   **Finding like-minded people.** An alternative way of using a 'likes'/'dislikes' round can be asking the students to find someone else in the group with similar likes and dislikes, and to form a duo or trio to prepare a poster or short sketch illustrating their shared feelings.

8   **Learning happens by doing.** To help you to get to know their names, once you have a complete list of the names, ask people from your list at random some (easy) questions. At first, you may need to keep your eyes on your list as you say someone's name, and wait till you hear where their voice is coming from before looking up at them. However, the more often you use their names, the easier you'll find it to look at the right person when using their name.

9   **Place cards?** In tutorials, laboratories and other places where small groups of students are positioned in particular places for a while, it is useful to give each student a 'place card' (a folded A5 sheet of card serves well – paper will do) and have them write their names on both sides of the card, and place the cards on the tables or benches (or at their feet if they are sitting without tables). Cards can be seen at a distance much better than labels. This allows you to address individuals by name, and also helps them to get to know each other's names.

10 **Make yourself a template?** When you know all the (preferred) names of members of a large group, make an overhead transparency with all the names on it, and use this to structure seminar groups or syndicate groups. Put a blank sheet of transparency on top of this template, and add (for example) letters A, B, C, D . . . beside names to divide the larger group into sub-groups, and perhaps put an asterisk beside the names of convenors (rotating such roles as successive tasks are issued). This gradually helps you get to know

all the names of students even in quite large groups (and allows you to retain your template for future use with this particular class). Seeing each other's names on the screen is a way of helping members of quite large groups not to feel so anonymous or 'lonely'.

12

Helping students to get the most from tutorials

Despite the fact that relatively little real learning happens during most lectures, students tend to regard lectures as more important than tutorials. This is compounded by the fact that many lecturers treat tutorials as relatively *ad hoc* occasions. The following suggestions may help you to deliver greater learning pay-off in your tutorials.

1   **Help students to see the purpose of tutorials.** Students with no higher education background in their family tradition may think that what is accepted as 'good behaviour' in school (for example, being quiet!) is what is expected of them in college settings too. Normally, the last thing you want your students to be in tutorials is passive.

2   **Avoid the temptation to use tutorials to elaborate on things that have been covered in lectures.** It is all too easy for tutorials to degenerate into an extension of lectures, and for students to be as passive in tutorials as they are in most lectures. Make it worth students' while to come to the tutorials: ensure they leave having achieved things that they otherwise would have missed.

3   **Have a definite purpose for each tutorial.** For example, link at least some tutorials with specific intended learning outcomes. Make it clear to students that there are parts of their programme which will be covered only in tutorials, and that these parts will be assessed in the same way as the lecture content of the programme.

4   **Let students know the agenda.** Whenever possible, brief students in advance concerning the topics to be processed in forthcoming tutorials. Give them something specific to prepare for each tutorial, and spend some of (but not all) the time letting them share and discuss what they have prepared. Always have something up your sleeve for students to do or discuss during tutorials for those occasions when none of the students brings questions or problems.

5   **Encourage students to make good use of tutorials to sort out things they don't yet understand.** Explain to students that tutorials are usually the best times to ask you detailed questions. Suggest that they jot down questions and issues as they arise, and bring their lists to each tutorial. Spend some time during each tutorial dealing with these questions or issues.

6   **Help students to capture the learning that happens in tutorials.** Give them suggestions to help them integrate the things you cover in tutorials with the rest of their experiences on the programme. For example, suggest they keep a tutorial learning log or diary to remind them of the main issues and questions that were dealt with during tutorials.

7   **Use tutorials to get feedback** on how students are finding lectures and practical work. Check whether or not they have mastered things that have been covered already. Have additional tasks and practice exercises to hand, which you can use during tutorials or issue to students to try on their own later.

8   **Use tutorials to help students work together.** Use tutorials for allowing students to bring forward the products of tasks they have undertaken collaboratively. When a tutorial group really gels, the students will often continue to work informally in the same group.

9   **Find out how students feel about your tutorials.** Ask students direct questions about how they are finding the tutorials. For example, by asking them to tell you what they would like you to 'stop doing', 'start doing' and 'continue doing', you can very quickly gain useful information to help you structure future tutorials.

10   **Use tutorials to bridge the gaps between different elements of a programme.** For example, use tutorials to draw together themes from quite different parts of the programme. It is often useful to invite colleagues in to contribute to specific tutorials when the need arises to weld links between interrelated topics.

13

Helping students to benefit from seminars

Some programmes have lectures, seminars and tutorials, and it's not always clear to students how these respective teaching–learning situations are different. Sometimes they don't feel different at all! Probably the main features that distinguish seminars from tutorials are that each seminar is planned around a definite topic or issue, and students are progressively expected to prepare themselves to take the lead in seminars.

1   **Help your students to see what seminars are meant to be.** Explain how they differ from tutorials and lectures. Students may not automatically know the educational functions that seminars can serve.

2   **Work out a seminar schedule and publish this along with your lecture schedule.** This can help students to see which topics or issues are going to be covered in depth in seminars.

3   **Brief students carefully.** As the programme progresses, brief individual students (or small groups) to prepare for forthcoming seminars – for example, to give a 15-minute review of a topic, then open it up for discussion (with you as an expert witness only when needed).

4   **Agree ground rules for seminars.** These can address such things as punctuality, contribution, preparation and record-keeping. If, for example, students take turns to prepare a short résumé of what was covered in seminars, each member of the group gradually builds up a supplementary set of learning resource materials.

5   **Don't let students' questions just vanish into the air.** When a seminar is being used for an in-depth discussion of something that students have covered in lectures (or from directed reading), facilitate the generation of a physical list of questions. This can be done by writing up students' questions on a flip chart or marker board (and can be done even more rapidly by

issuing Post-it™ notes to everyone and asking them to write their questions concisely and put them up for display).

6   **Consider making seminars count towards overall assessment.** This helps students to take them more seriously. Furthermore, the smaller groups involved in seminars can more easily participate in self-assessment and peer assessment processes, giving students the chance to gain a feel about the sort of assessment criteria that may be involved in other coursework assessment, and exams too.

7   **Allow sufficient time for preparation, especially if the seminars are being assessed.** Where individual students or groups are being assessed on the basis of their contributions to seminars (for example, giving presentations, tabling a paper, leading a discussion), give them adequate time to prepare their contributions, and clarify the way the seminars will be conducted and assessed – for example, by a printed briefing sheet or checklist.

8   **Make the most of student ownership of seminars.** Use seminar sessions to build flexibility into the overall programme. For example, give students choices from which to select the exact topics and formats of their forthcoming contributions. It can often help to invite an 'expert witness' from outside the programme to contribute to particular seminars that students themselves have requested – indeed, the students themselves can be given the task of finding such a person.

9   **Consider bringing in more experienced students.** It can be useful to bring in (for example) third-year students to lead a series of seminars with first-year students. The more experienced students can often explain things in a more understandable way than someone like yourself, who has probably 'known them for a long time'. Additionally, explaining things to less experienced students is one of the best ways of deepening the more experienced students' own understanding of the topics they're explaining.

10 **Try to keep everyone involved.** The student(s) leading a seminar are of course already involved, as are those asking questions later, but it is desirable to make sure that everyone present thinks and learns too. For example, involve other students in writing questions (or conclusions) on pieces of paper or overhead transparencies, to overcome the problem of some students talking too much while others hardly talk at all.

11 **Feed back seminars into lectures when possible.** Too often, a seminar programme can seem to students simply to be an extension of a lecture programme, but it can work the other way too. For example, use seminars on specific topics to generate lists of students' questions and problems to use as the basis for a forthcoming large-group lecture.

14

Helping students to make the most of small-group sessions

Small-group teaching and learning is less 'public' than large-group lectures, but it can be every bit as important for students. Many tutors and lecturers find it an uphill struggle to get students to contribute to small-group sessions, whether seminars or tutorials. It seems that as long as a tutor is prepared to talk, students will gladly listen. Here we list some suggestions about ways of helping to ensure that students play a more active role in small-group contexts.

1 **Recognise that some students may be quite shy.** Avoid bullying them into participation in small-group sessions, especially near the beginning of a programme, when they may be feeling insecure and when even slight embarrassment may be taken too seriously.

2 **Use icebreakers to help students to get to know each other.** Get them talking to each other using non-threatening situations. There are dozens of icebreakers you can choose from. Better still, develop your own – ones that really work with your own students. Build up your stock of short, informal tasks and exercises so that you can regularly start off a small-group session in an informal or 'fun' way.

3 **Brief your students carefully.** When it is intended that students are to make substantial contributions to a particular small-group session, give them a helpful briefing at least the week before, so that anyone who is nervous has the opportunity to do adequate preparation and will feel more at ease about the prospect of contributing.

4 **Explain the benefits of small-group work to students.** Discuss with students the value they can derive from such contexts, and particularly help them to see that the more they contribute to the sessions, the more they will learn themselves. Remind them how important it will be for their future careers to develop their interpersonal communication skills, and explain how small-group teaching and learning contexts are ideal for this.

5   **Emphasise the importance of small-group learning contexts.** Ensure that students don't fall into the trap of thinking that because such sessions are less formal than lectures, they are less important. In lectures, explain from time to time that 'the important issues here will form the basis of your seminars and tutorials in the next week or two'.

6   **Allow students to play to their strengths in small-group contexts.** For example, let students to participate in different ways in seminars and tutorials. Some will readily talk and discuss, while others will prefer to prepare a hand-out, poster or overhead transparency to constitute their contribution to a small-group session.

7   **Make the most of sub-groups.** For example, divide the larger group of students into discussion groups of four or five for (say) 15 minutes, then allow volunteers from each group to report back in whatever format they prefer to use: orally, or using a flip chart or slide (giving a suggested maximum time for each report back).

8   **Work with the art of the possible.** Establish, with the students, some ground rules for contributions to small-group sessions. Help students to work out practical criteria that the group can adopt. When the ownership of the ground rules rests with the students themselves, they are more likely to try to live up to the criteria, not least of which can be that everyone contributes in an appropriate way.

9   **Don't let anyone drown.** There should be no personal humiliation. Come quickly to the rescue if particular students seem seriously uncomfortable as they contribute to a small-group session. Get to know which ones are 'robust' enough to weather any difficulties, and which ones will appreciate your helpful intervention.

10 **Mix and match the group membership.** Consider the possibilities of having more than one kind of small group. For example, you could use 'home groups' as an ongoing support-building process throughout the programme, and differently constituted 'task groups' for particular topics or purposes. This helps avoid the problems that can occur when a particular group does not 'gel', as it is then not the only group that each of its members works in.

15

Helping students to make the most of each other

In practice, students often find that they learn at least as much from each other as from any other source (including the Internet, reference materials and tutors). However, they often feel that somehow they're not intended to cooperate actively with each other as part of their day-to-day learning strategy. The following suggestions may help them change this view.

1   **Show students how much they learn from their peers.** Remind them that they have access to their peers for many more hours per week than they have access to 'expert witnesses' such as lecturers or tutors.

2   **Point out the value of 'informal' groups.** Spontaneously formed groups can often address problems that are common to most members of the group (including parts of subjects everyone is having difficulty with). By putting their heads together, the members of a group can more quickly find a way of addressing a problem.

3   **Equip students with tools that can help them work together.** For example, suggest that students in peer-support groups do a 'SWOT' (strengths, weaknesses, opportunities, threats) analysis, identifying the total strengths and weaknesses of the group, working out what opportunities there are for the group to be a useful part of the learning processes of its members, and working out what threats the group as a whole perceives (as a first step to devising ways of countering the threats).

4   **Help students to take stock of their resources.** Encourage peer-support groups to make an inventory of what's available to them to help them to succeed, including tutors, students in the next year up, counsellors and advisers, and online, textual or computer-based resources.

5   **Point out the benefits of sharing problems.** Point out how valuable peer-support groups can be when members have individual or personal problems.

It can be much less threatening to share such problems with some reasonably close friends than to bring them to the notice of a tutor. Often, members of the group can provide all the help and support that may be needed. Alternatively, members of the group can advise when a problem really does need some expert help.

6   **Develop some case studies of successful peer support.** Try to identify some students (past or present) who have found peer-support groups particularly valuable. Ask them to provide case-study evidence about how they used their group, and what sorts of problems the group successfully handled. The evidence could be presented in person to a class, or as a video, or as a short written case study. Some such case studies could be useful material to include in your next student handbook.

7   **Respect students' choices.** Accept that some students will prefer to maintain their independence and privacy, and will resent any attempt to force them to participate in informal peer-support groups. If such students are manipulated into joining such groups, they can have a damaging effect on the group. Allow students the choice of whether or not to engage in peer-support networks (possibly even suggesting that those who wish to maintain their independence and distance form their own like-minded group).

8   **Consider offering alternative assessed tasks.** When devising coursework tasks and assignments, think whether you can offer choices to students, including tasks designed to be done as group exercises as well as tasks designed for independent work. Remember, however, that it is important for students not to feel that they may have been disadvantaged by the choice they made.

9   **Build teams.** Try out some team-building exercises in seminars and tutorials, allowing students to see for themselves the different roles that can be played by members of an effective team. Encourage students to put what they learn about teamwork into practice in their own ways, and remind them how important such skills are likely to be to future employers.

10 **Capture what goes wrong and turn it to everyone's advantage.** With the best will in the world, not everything goes right with group work every time! Build up a bank of 'students' problems' scenarios. Spend a little time giving groups of students 'a problem' and asking them to work out a plan of action to overcome the problem. Give each group a different problem, to avoid the report-back stage becoming repetitive. Ask students to contribute (anonymously if they wish) to the bank of problems for future use.

16

Helping students to learn from each other

Students need encouragement to capitalise on the fact that they can learn a great deal from each other. Indeed, they may take some convincing that they can learn even more from each other than from you! The competitive culture often prevents them from deriving maximum benefit from each other, yet a group always has a greater amount of knowledge, experience and competence than its individual members.

1 **Encourage the formation of study syndicates.** If these are formed spontaneously by students, there is the benefit of ownership of the group by the students comprising it. The aim of a study syndicate should be along the lines of 'each and every member will do better than they would have on their own'.

2 **Promote the benefits of being skilled in group work.** These include the development of leadership skills and the taking of responsibility for their own actions. The benefits also include the development of the ability to be led – 'followership' – which in the context of working with others is just as important an attribute as leadership.

3 **Provide time for study syndicates to work.** For example, if formal classes run from 9 a.m. to 10 a.m., then 11 a.m. to 12 noon, groups can work independently from 10 to 11 a.m., both on tasks arising from the earlier class and on matters coming up in the subsequent one.

4 **Provide space suitable for study syndicate work.** At its simplest, a table and chairs are all that groups require – preferably in a room where groups can make some noise (not a typical library). Accessories such as blackboards, whiteboards or flip charts can help the groups to focus their activities.

5 **Help students to distinguish between collaboration and cheating.** Learning from other members of the group should be regarded as productive.

The only activity that should be regarded as cheating is failure to make an appropriate contribution to the work of the group in assessment-related contexts.

6 **Encourage students to learn by assessing each other's efforts and giving each other feedback.** Help them to identify the criteria by which they can assess each other's work. Applying assessment criteria is an excellent way to deepen learning, and also helps students to tune into the assessment culture that surrounds their work on the pathway towards their qualifications.

7 **Encourage students to quiz each other.** Rapid informal practice at answering questions is excellent practice for answering questions in more formal situations such as written or oral exams. Students answering each other's questions are less likely to be able to 'con' themselves about which questions they can answer than are students working by themselves.

8 **Provide opportunities for students to teach each other.** The act of explaining something to someone else is one of the most powerful ways of learning, with a high level of learning pay-off. If each member of the group explains a selected topic to the rest of the group, the total learning achieved by the group is maximised.

9 **Ask groups of students to brainstorm questions.** Identifying the right questions is often more than halfway towards being able to answer them effectively. Ask groups to prioritise their lists of questions. Where some questions require the expert assistance of the teacher, it can be comforting to students that the questions have a degree of anonymity, belonging to the group rather than to particular individuals.

10 **Devise some tasks that are best done by groups rather than by individuals.** Break tasks into a number of complementary parts, where bringing together the parts can occur naturally in groups. This helps students to recognise the importance of teamwork, and equips them to demonstrate their competence at working with others to (for example) prospective employers.

17

Helping students to find and use mentors

A mentor is sometimes defined as 'a trusted colleague'. An alternative way of thinking of a mentor is 'someone who has already done something' helping 'someone who is just starting to do it'. It can be highly profitable for students to find themselves a mentor and make good use of such a person. Here are some suggestions.

1   **Tell students how useful it is to have someone who can be 'on their side' always.** Explain that (particularly with large numbers of students) the tutor–student relationship is necessarily not quite as 'personal' as can be a mentor–student relationship. Therefore, it is useful for students to seek some other person who can 'help to keep them going, especially when the going gets tough'.

2   **Point out the value of a neutral third party.** It is worth thinking about the conflict that sometimes arises for academic staff between tutoring, advising and assessing. This can limit the amount of help tutors can be seen to give students. A neutral 'third party' such as a mentor is able to give help and advice even on sensitive areas such as assessment.

3   **Show students the sorts of people whom they could consider for the role of mentor.** Explain to students the different sorts of 'mentor' they may wish to choose from. For example, mature students may already have a spouse or partner who is in an ideal position to fulfil the role of a mentor. Part-time students may have supervisors or managers who can make very effective mentors. First-year students may know someone from a more advanced stage of the programme who is willing to act as a mentor for them. A good mentor is simply anyone who can do what's most needed.

4   **Get students to work out the roles a mentor could play for them:** for example, 'someone to moan to', 'someone to go to when the going is tough', 'someone to help when decisions are to be made', 'simply someone who will

listen', 'someone who's been there before and who will offer advice', 'someone who can step in and help solve problems', and so on. Different students need different kinds of mentor.

5   **What's in it for your mentor?** Get students to work out how they can make mentoring a two-way beneficial exchange. For many mentors, the satisfaction of feeling that they are giving useful help will be enough. Other mentors may need to feel that they are investing in people, and that their mentoring work is evidence of this.

6   **Remember that mentors may need some training.** If you are in a position to arrange a 'supply' of potential mentors (for example, if you can enlist some third-year students to mentor first-year students), it can be worthwhile to arrange a mentor training workshop, helping mentors to work out the sorts of things they can help with, and also when *not* to try to help (such as with those personal problems that could need expert help).

7   **Get into it yourself!** Probably the best way to get a feel for mentoring is to be a mentor, and to have one. Many organisations now use mentoring systems of one kind or another for newcomers to the staff. Consider whether you could be involved in something similar in your own department or organisation.

8   **Counsel about competitive tendencies.** Alert students to the dangers of the 'competitive culture' they may have come from. The education system often tends to condition students to try to work on their own, whereas in the world of work, employers want people who can get on well with each other. Mentoring is a useful process for developing interpersonal and social skills for both mentors and students.

9   **Help students to agree appropriate ground rules with their mentors.** It can be useful for mentors and students to work to an ongoing negotiated agreement regarding their respective roles and responsibilities. Suggest that students can draw up proposals for their part of such an agreement, and offer these to mentors.

10 **Don't make mentoring mandatory.** Despite all the advantages of mentoring, accept that there will be some students who simply do not wish to enter into this sort of arrangement. If they remain unconvinced of the benefits, their right to learn in their own independent way needs to be respected.

18

Being an expert witness

This section is about helping your students to learn from *you*: not just as a tutor, but as someone who has already succeeded – in other words, an expert witness. With increasing recognition of the value of learning by doing, the role of tutors has changed from that of being 'founts of knowledge' to that of being facilitators of learning. Some put this by saying that 'the sage on the stage is now the guide by your side'. However, if tutors are to be as helpful to students as possible, it is useful for them to be available as a learning resource at suitable times and in suitable ways.

1   **Make yourself available to answer students' questions.** The simplest way of being an expert witness is to be available to sort out the questions that students come up with. Since it is not normally possible to answer questions very efficiently in large-group teaching–learning situations, it is worth using one or more of the suggestions below to 'collect and focus' the questions, so that you can help students towards answers.

2   **Take them down in writing and use them as evidence.** Taking written questions is a useful process when large groups of students are involved. For example, you can advise that at the end of the lecture you would like slips of paper or Post-it™ notes with written questions (with students' names, or anonymously if they prefer) to be passed forward to you, and that you will deal with these at the beginning of the next large-group session.

3   **Look for the frequently asked questions.** When armed with a set of questions collected as above, you can expect that there will be considerable overlaps between questions. It's worth finding the three most common questions and preparing a question–answer slide or handout so that students are able to capture your answers to the main questions.

4   **Make use of the odd questions too.** When named individuals supply you with 'minority' questions, it can be worth waiting till you have the

chance to answer them directly to the people concerned (for example, in a tutorial, or one-to-one interview) rather than giving the large group your answer.

5   **Build time for questions and answers into tutorials and other small-group contexts.** You may wish to use tutorials for dealing with all questions from students. A disadvantage of this is that students from other tutorial groups may not benefit from your 'expert witness' answers to one particular group. It can therefore be worth making a log of 'questions asked and answered' in tutorials, and make these available to all students – for example, online or as handout material.

6   **Don't just answer any questions.** Sometimes you may want students to go off and research for themselves the answers to some questions, especially those that are linked to assessed coursework. It can be useful to establish some ground rules regarding the sorts of questions you are willing to answer, as opposed to those questions where you really intend students to go about finding their own answers without your help.

7   **Consider scheduling 'expert witness' occasions.** When setting project work, seminar preparation, and so on, you may wish to be available to each group in an 'expert witness' capacity at certain stages. This may be restricted to particular phases of the work (for example, when an action plan for the project work has been made). Alternatively, you could arrange to be available at a particular time for consultation.

8   **Remember that your expertise is not just in the subject matter.** A further important area of your expertise is to do with the fact that you yourself have learned the subject successfully. How best to go about learning particular aspects of your subject is useful information to make available to students.

9   **Share your expertise with other tutors and their students.** When it is possible for you to work with colleagues in team-teaching processes, it is often useful for you to be 'expert witness' for a colleague's group of students, and vice versa. This can help students to benefit from the different perspectives that tutors necessarily have by helping them to gain a more balanced overall view.

10   **Students' learning is usually driven by assessment.** The most direct ways that students will use you as an 'expert witness' are normally in connection with assessment of their work – coursework and/or examinations. Many other suggestions in this book are intended to help you share your expertise with students in the context of assessment.

11   **Let your students know about what you've published.** They may be able to use some of this material as an extra resource. It also helps to enhance your own credibility with them, and helps them to perceive your worth as an expert witness.

Chapter 3

The programme itself: lectures, assignments and feedback

Next we offer an assortment of suggestions relating to some of the main processes used in teaching and learning, ranging from lectures to written work. As is the case throughout this book, we do not intend merely to provide 'teaching tips' as such; rather, we have tried to offer suggestions regarding how students themselves can be led towards increased success and effectiveness in the various tasks and situations they meet.

19

Helping students to make the most of your lectures

Students normally regard lectures as very important, yet during them they tend to be passive, and poor 'receivers' if they are allowed to remain passive. The following suggestions can help students approach your lectures more proactively.

1 **Make good use of the intended learning outcomes.** Show the intended learning outcomes to be addressed in the lecture as a slide near the beginning of the lecture, and return to this slide near the end so that students are reminded what *they* should be achieving as a result of the lecture.

2 **Keep reminding students of the big picture.** For example, towards the end of each lecture, let students know what will be coming up in the *next* lecture. It can be useful to give them a plan of a whole set of lectures, learning outcomes included. Suggest that students (individually or in groups) brainstorm what they already know about the topic before coming to the lecture.

3 **Build upon what students already know.** Sometimes, at the start of a lecture allow a few minutes for students to privately brainstorm their answers to 'what I already know about . . . '. A further way of helping students to tune in to your lecture is to display last year's exam question on the topic of the lecture, at the beginning or end of the lecture, so that students are alerted regarding what they may be expected to do with the content.

4 **Find out what students really want.** Suggest sometimes at the start of a lecture that groups of students brainstorm 'what we want to find out today about . . . '. Alternatively, issue Post-it™ notes to the students and ask them to jot down headlines following on from 'what I really want from this lecture is . . . '. Use the results of such brainstorms as an agenda for your lecture, making sure that you address as many as possible of the things students want from the event.

5   **Encourage students to review the content of each lecture.** For example, ask them to decide what they would write down as 'the one thing I really need to remember from this lecture' or 'the three most important points mentioned today'. Suggest that they do this individually, then compare their decisions with those of some other students.

6   **Help students to make better notes.** Point out the benefits of *making* notes, rather than simply *taking* notes. Explain how easy it is to be mentally quite passive if just writing down the words they hear or see on the screen, whereas it is possible to be much more active by putting ideas and concepts into their own words as the lecture proceeds.

7   **Help students to get down to following up lectures.** Suggest that they allocate a few minutes two or three days later to process each lecture systematically, by jotting on one side of a small card the key issues covered by the lecture, and on the reverse some questions they need to become able to answer about the content of the lecture.

8   **Encourage students to discuss lectures.** Suggest that students spend a few minutes in a small group reviewing each lecture, using the notes and questions they prepared while reviewing it individually. During this group review, students can add each other's questions and summary points to their own collections, so that each member of the group leaves with better resources than he or she started with.

9   **Find out what students have learned from previous lectures.** From time to time, give out Post-it™ notes to the whole group during a lecture and ask everyone to write on them three or more questions covered by past lectures, which they think it is important to be able to answer. Stick the Post-its™ on a wall, and 'tour' the agenda of questions, giving your own (authoritative) comments regarding the relative importance of particular questions.

10 **Help students to map their learning.** Now and then, use some time in lectures or tutorials to ask groups of students to create mind maps of the content of the lecture programme to date. This can help them to see how the various topics link together, and reminds them of what they are expected to have learned already.

11 **Get quick (and sharp) feedback during your programme of lectures.** One way is to give out Post-it™ notes and ask students to write the heading words 'stop', 'start' and 'continue' across the top of them, then tell you things they would like you to do under each heading. The Post-its™ can be stuck anonymously to a wall. The 'stop' entries will often alert you to things you had no idea were amiss. The 'start' entries can alert you to things that you can address in the next few lectures. The 'continue' entries are the good news.

45

Stop . . .	Start . . .	Continue . . .

20

How *not* to lecture!

Sometimes it's even more useful to spotlight things that go badly than to try to advise on what to do well. Unlike most of the tips in this book, this set is written in reverse – based on 20 things that cause students grief in some of their lectures. You may wish to share these tips on lecturing with your students, who almost certainly will be able to add one or two that are even more relevant to your own subject discipline – and perhaps indeed to your own lecturing.

1 **Read out your notes carefully to students.** This means you can be sure they write down a good set of notes, and also that you will have covered everything that you covered last year.

2 **Don't read your notes out too quickly.** Your students need to be thinking about what they're writing, so make sure that you leave long pauses between sentences so that they can get their heads around your words of wisdom. Sometimes they close their eyes while thinking deeply between sentences, so use this as a measure that you've got your pace just right.

3 **Don't tell students about the intended learning outcomes for your lecture.** They'll only grumble if they can't work out what the outcomes actually mean, and they'll grumble even more if you choose to miss something out because you didn't want to say anything about it.

4 **Don't let students get away with coming in late.** Have a supply of cutting comments to direct at offenders such as 'couldn't get out of bed this morning?' or 'so nice of you to come and join us'. This discourages students from coming in late and teaches them to be polite to you, and they won't be a nuisance in future.

5   **Try to avoid eye contact with students.** Students can become frightened that you may ask them questions if you look directly at them, so concentrate on looking at your notes, your feet, the ceiling and the back wall of the room.

6   **Don't speak too loudly or too clearly.** You need to keep the students on their toes in your lecture. Those sitting at the front are the keen ones and will hear what you say. Those sitting at the back don't really care very much about your subject, and have already decided to fail your exam.

7   **Try to avoid having colleagues sitting in on your lectures**. They are likely to be critical and awkward, especially if they've just completed a postgraduate certificate in academic practice or suchlike. It's your lecture, and you know the subject, so what else matters?

8   **Don't worry if audience numbers decrease as your lecture programme continues.** Some students will decide that they're not up to the subject, and those who come will not then be held up by them. Also, if numbers taking the exam are low, this means you can take more care marking the answers of those students who really care.

9   **Check out whether any of your students have special needs.** Ask for a show of hands about which students are dyslexic, which have mental health problems and which can't see you properly. Not many will indicate any special need, so you can confidently continue knowing that you've addressed this issue.

10   **Dim the lights when you're showing slides.** This helps students to see your slides more clearly, and gives you a breather from being the focus of their attention. It also makes sure that students are thinking deeply about your slides rather than trying to make notes about them.

11   **Don't give your students copies of your slides.** They will just switch off and take no notice of what you are telling them if they've got their own copies of your slides. Or worse, they will nitpick and ask you questions about what's on your slides. Keep them learning by doing – writing out your slides for themselves.

12   **Make full use of the screen.** Put plenty of information onto slides. The students at the front will get full value from your slides. Those further back aren't keen on your subject and probably won't pass the module anyway, so concentrate on the students at the front.

13 **Don't be too slow with your slides.** The brighter students will copy them down quickly, so don't wait till everyone has finished writing. After all, your job is to sort out the bright students from the rest.

14 **Be careful when students interrupt you to ask questions.** They're probably trying to slow you down or catch you out. You can minimise such behaviours by turning the tables and asking them awkward questions yourself.

15 **Make full use of your allotted time.** If it's ten minutes late when you get started, because someone else was over-running in the room before you, it's only fair that you continue that extra ten minutes to get through all your material. The students won't mind this.

16 **Don't worry if students look puzzled or bemused.** This simply means that you've pitched your lecture at the right level – after all, there's no point in telling them about things they can already understand; that would just bore them.

17 **Don't tell students anything about what's coming up in the exam.** This will just distract them from absorbing your lecture, and the bright ones will already know what to revise.

18 **Don't put too much into any handouts you use.** If the handouts are complete in themselves, students won't turn up to your lectures and will just copy the handouts from those who did attend. If you use no handouts at all, this problem is completely solved.

19 **Always ask 'any questions?' at the end of your lecture.** There won't usually be any, and if there are, you can always refer them to the set textbook, but students do like to be asked if they have any questions, and if you don't ask for questions they will grumble about it on the module evaluation forms later.

20 **Don't ask students for feedback on your lectures.** They've got more important things to do than fill in questionnaires. You'll find out how well (or how badly) they did soon enough when their exam results are worked out. So will they.

21

What *not* to do with PowerPoint™!

Any presentation medium can be used well or badly. Most lecture theatres and many large teaching classrooms are nowadays equipped for Microsoft Power-Point™ presentation – where you bring in your laptop (or floppy disk or CD-ROM or memory stick), get yourself hitched up to a data projector (often ceiling mounted), and off you go (or at least so you hope!). The following *don'ts* may help you make this presentation work well for you – and for your students.

1   **Don't underestimate the problems that can arise.** You may not be able to get the room dark enough for students to see your presentation properly. There may be compatibility problems between the software version you have used to create your presentation, and the version on the computer through which you wish to show it. The image size on your laptop may not be compatible with that required by the data projector. The resolution of the projection equipment may not be sufficient to show fine details of images that you carefully placed into your presentation.

2   **Don't overdo the special effects.** Doing the whole presentation in a single format becomes boring for your audience, but programming a random sequence of slide builds tends to be irritating for you as presenter, as you don't know what build sequence will be produced when you move to your next slide. Similarly, don't go overboard on the snazzy changes from one slide to the next. And don't cause 'death by bullet point'! PowerPoint™ can introduce bullet points to slides in a variety of ways (fly from left, dissolve, and so on), but too many bullet points can quickly become tiresome to an audience.

3   **Don't use it just like an overhead projector substitute!** Simply transferring the contents of your overhead transparencies into a computer-delivered presentation does not make full use of the medium. Try to do *other* things with computer-aided presentations – for example, making good use of the possibilities of moving images, graphics, and so on.

4 **Don't forget that it's not that bright!** Except in well-equipped lecture theatres with dimmable lighting (and blinds on any windows there may be), the projection equipment may not be nearly as bright as a good overhead projector. This means that in most other teaching rooms you may need to take particular care with room lighting, daylight from windows and (worst of all) direct sunlight.

5 **Don't forget the conditions appropriate for human sleep!** Turning down the lights, sitting comfortably in the same place for more than a few minutes, and listening to the sound of your voice may be just the right conditions for your students to drop off, particularly if the images are unclear.

6 **Don't put too much on any slide.** There still seem to be few computer-aided presentations in which *all* the slides are perfectly readable from the back of the room. It is better to have twice as many slides than to cram lots of information onto each slide. It usually takes two or more slides to project the same amount of information that would have taken one overhead transparency.

7 **Don't put important things in the lower half of slides.** Unless all members of your audience have an uninterrupted view of the screen, people sitting at the back may have to peer around their nearer neighbours to see what's at the bottom of the screen. Unlike with overhead projection, you can't simply move a transparency up the platen to make the final points visible to people at the back.

8 **Don't import tables or text files.** The fact that you *can* import such files into a computer-managed presentation package leads many into temptation. These are very often the slides that can't be read from the back (or even from the front). It is normally better to give students such information as handouts than to try to show them it on screen.

9 **Don't use the wrong colours.** Colours that look good on a computer screen don't always show up so well when they are projected. If most of your presentations will be in rooms with natural daylight, it is usually best to stick to dark colours for text, and light (or even white) backgrounds. If you know you're going to be working in a lecture theatre where you have full control of the lighting, you can then be more adventurous and use light lettering against dark backgrounds (but not forgetting that you may be lulling your audience to sleep when you turn down the lights).

10 **Don't leave a slide on when you've moved on to talk about something else.** It is better to switch the projection off rather than to leave up information that people have already thought about. If you're within reach of the computer keyboard, pressing 'B' on some systems causes the displ.

to go black, and pressing 'B' again brings the display back instantly. This is far simpler and safer than switching the projector to standby, and risking having to wait for it to warm up again when you want to project your next slide. An alternative is to insert a 'black' slide when you wish to stop your audience from looking at the screen. Don't, however, forget where you've placed this, and panic about where your display has gone!

11   **Don't talk to the screen!** With overhead projectors it's easy to develop good habits, including looking at the transparency rather than at the screen and avoiding turning your back on your audience. With projected images you may have no alternative but to watch the screen, but you need to make sure that you talk to your audience. If you can arrange things so that you can look at a computer screen rather than the projection screen, the problem can be partly solved.

12   **Don't underestimate the potential of remote controls surprising you!** Many systems allow you to change slides with a remote control connected to your computer, or to the projection equipment. Pressing the wrong button on this can switch the system to something quite different (for example, video input), and can mean that you can find yourself unable to get back to your presentation without losing your cool. It is best to find out in advance which buttons *not* to press, and possibly to place some adhesive tape over them to reduce the possibility of pressing them.

13   **Don't forget your overheads!** It is still useful to have at least some of your computer slides on traditional transparencies. Computers can go down. More likely, you can still press the wrong button on a remote control, and switch your projector onto video or off altogether. At such times it can seem life-saving to be able to go back to overhead projector, at least temporarily.

22

Making the most of the overhead projector

Though PowerPoint™ and data-projection facilities are now standard equipment in most lecture theatres and many large classrooms, overhead projectors remain a common way of displaying visual information to students in most teaching rooms. An advantage of overhead projection is that there is much less to go wrong, and it needs little time to set up. Several of our suggestions about PowerPoint™ continue to apply to using overhead projectors well. The following additional guidelines, adapted from *Lecturing: A Practical Guide*, may help your students get the most from your use of the overhead projector.

1 **Make good-looking transparencies.** Good-quality overheads can add credibility to your messages. It's worth using desktop publishing programs (or indeed PowerPoint™ software itself) to make your principal overhead transparencies look professional and believable. With ink-jet and laser colour printers it's nowadays relatively easy to produce coloured transparencies with graphics.

2 **Be careful with coloured print or writing.** Some colours, especially red, are harder to see from the back of a large room than you might imagine. Throw away any orange or yellow ones from your set of overhead pens – unless you're using them for colouring in blocks on diagrams or flowcharts, for example.

3 **Don't use typewritten overheads.** To be clearly visible, most fonts need to be at sizes '18', '24' or larger – considerably bigger and bolder than typical typewritten materials. Make sure that each transparency you prepare will be visible from the back of the largest room you are likely to use, even by someone without good eyesight.

4 **Watch students' eyes.** As soon as you notice students having to move their head positions to see something on one of your transparencies, it's worth trying to move that part up so that they can see it without moving their gaze.

Use the top half of the screen. By sliding your transparencies up, you can normally make the most important pieces of information appear towards the top of the screen – more easily visible by students at your sessions.

5   **Get your transparencies into the right order before your lecture.** There's nothing worse than watching a lecturer sifting and sorting to try to find the right overhead. It's sometimes worth arranging them into two sets: ones you will *definitely* use, and ones you *might* wish to use if time permits, or if anticipated questions arise.

6   **Try not to read out your overheads word for word!** Your students can usually read much faster than you can speak. People don't like having things read out to them that they can read for themselves. However, if there are people in your audience who *need* to hear what's on your slides, for example because of visual impairment, you may have to read them out.

7   **Minimise passive transcribing by students.** Copying down words from transparencies is not the most productive of learning activities. Where possible, issue handout materials that already contain the wording from your principal overhead transparencies.

8   **Be prepared to add things to your transparencies during discussions.** The ability to edit slides 'live' is an advantage of overhead projectors over computer-based presentation managers (unless you are a very skilled and confident PowerPoint™ user), and can help your students to feel that their comments are important and valued. With transparencies produced from ink-jet printers, however, don't write on your original (you can often damage the ink on the original slide); instead, put a blank sheet of acetate over it.

9   **Don't overuse 'progressive reveal' techniques** (showing transparencies a bit at a time by gradually moving a masking sheet of paper). Some students feel manipulated if they are continually 'controlled' in this way. It can be better to build up a complex overhead using multiple overlays.

10   **Remember to switch the projector off!** Most overhead projectors make at least some noise. When you're not actually showing something, it's important that you are not distracting your students both visually and auditorily.

11   **Always carry some spare overhead transparencies and pens.** These can be used for interactive tasks, such as asking students in groups to write up questions that can then be displayed and shared with the whole group. Students feel a greater sense of ownership of their questions when their handwriting is displayed on the screen for all to see.

23

Compensating for other people's bad teaching!

It would be a strange world if every teacher were 'perfect', and all lectures, tutorials, seminars and laboratory classes were deep and enjoyable learning experiences. Assuming you've done your best to serve your own students as well as you can, you may still need to help them overcome the shortcomings of colleagues of yours. Indeed, if you're warm, friendly and approachable, you're quite likely to have students coming up and telling you about parts of their learning experience that are far less happy than your own contributions. Obviously this is a sensitive situation, but we hope the following suggestions may help.

1   **Encourage students to form self-help groups.** Among other things, they can use these to compensate for bad teaching. When several students put their heads together, they can often find ways of developing their understanding of the subjects concerned.

2   **Where possible, take part in team-teaching situations.** For example, sit in on colleagues' lectures and then run tutorials with their students (and vice versa). You may be surprised how useful it can be to witness other people's ways of teaching – learning both things to emulate and things to avoid. Team-teaching situations are one of the least threatening ways for you to demonstrate good-practice techniques that some of your colleagues may need to develop themselves.

3   **Spread the load.** Do what you can to arrange the teaching in your department so that students experience a variety of teaching styles. This is preferable to the possibility of some groups of students being overdosed in any one style (especially a difficult one).

4   **Help students to take more responsibility for their own learning.** You can assist by building in appropriate study-skills advice in your own sessions, or giving out study-skills aids. The more students can gain control over the ways they learn, the less susceptible to 'bad teaching' they become. Where

bad teaching has led to unproductive learning habits, take time with your students to alert them to the dangers they may be in. Help them identify hang-ups that they have been left with because of their unsatisfactory experiences.

5   **Be seen to collect feedback on your own teaching, and to act on it.** If you show colleagues how useful feedback can be in developing your own teaching style, they may be more ready to develop their own teaching in the same way. Be ready to tell colleagues about changes you made in your own approaches based on feedback from students.

6   **Help students to bridge the gaps.** When students have had unsatisfactory teaching of material that is a prerequisite to your own work with them, it may save you much time and energy in the long run to prepare an introductory learning package to help get them to the point you wish them to have reached before you start your own work with them. Such a package could be used instead of one or two of your timetabled sessions with them, so that they could catch up at their own pace and in their own ways (preferably working in informal groups where possible).

7   **Learn from other people's bad teaching!** Learning through mistakes is a perfectly valid way of learning, but it can be even better to learn from other people's mistakes! Try to find out exactly what your students regard as the hallmarks of 'bad teaching' and check that you're avoiding them yourself.

8   **Keep out of trouble!** Don't be tempted to criticise colleagues even if students tell you dreadful things about what they've been through in their sessions. Concentrate on ways that the students can be helped to compensate for whatever is missing in those parts of the teaching that are lacking in quality.

9   **Take part in departmental seminars about teaching and learning.** Give examples of things that have gone well in your own teaching – and (even better) things that did not go well at first, and what you did to improve the situation. Take care that the finger of blame is not pointed at whoever most needs to take note of your contributions to such seminars.

10   **Share teaching–learning resources you have made.** Contributing to a bank of handouts, PowerPoint™ presentations, overhead transparencies or a set of assignment questions can be useful ways of spreading your own good practice and helping colleagues to learn from it.

24

Helping students to *make* notes – not just *take* notes

Students spend a significant amount of time writing notes. However, often they are 'taking' notes (a passive, reproductive process) rather than 'making' notes (an active, decision-making process). The following ideas may help you to help your students to bring high learning pay-off to their writing of notes.

1 **Counsel students about how little they gain by simply copying down information.** Remind students how passive it is just to write down the words they hear in lectures, or the words they see on screens or boards, or indeed the words they read in a book. It is quite possible to write page after page in such a way without ever really thinking about what the words actually mean.

2 **Suggest to students that their own words can be better than anyone else's.** Suggest that in all forms of note-making they try to put ideas and concepts into their own words (except of course when they need to write down something verbatim – perhaps a definition or a quotation). This automatically engages their brains in working out what the words may mean, and how best to capture the meaning in their own words.

3 **Help your students to see the difference between information and knowledge.** As Einstein is reputed to have said, 'Knowledge is experience; everything else is just information.' If all students needed were the *information*, then handouts or printed copies of your lecture slides would be all they would need to take away from your lectures. The act of *making* notes during your lectures is the first stage in getting them to process the information, a step towards turning the information into their own knowledge.

4 **Help your students to make their notes look interesting.** Many students seem to have been taught to be economical with paper! They feel that they have to fill each page up uniformly, starting at the top left-hand corner and working down to the bottom right-hand corner. Remind students that if every page of their notes looks similar, they will be missing out on the strong 'visual'

side of their thinking. Making structured notes – mind maps, for example – is a way of using both verbal and visual memory and interpretation.

5   **Get students looking for what's really important in printed materials.** When everything in books or handouts is in the same size of print, it can sometimes be hard for students to pick out the vital information from the background information. Suggest that they search for and capture the shades of importance of different ideas, and translate them into something visual in their notes: different colours, different sizes of writing, boxes, and so on.

6   **Suggest that students write down *their* questions and *their* comments.** Advise them to interweave these with notes they make. For example, in lectures, many students *think* of questions they would like to find the answers to, but after an hour or two the questions have evaporated from their memories. When the questions are actually written into their notes, they then have the opportunity to go about seeking the answers.

7   **Encourage students to follow up each element of their note-making within a couple of days.** Suggest that students 'do something' with their notes, regularly, rather than just pile them up on a shelf. When they process their notes within a day or two, much of their original thinking at the time of note-making will come back to them. Making summaries, making additions, adding new topics, deciding what the most important points are – all these are all ways of turning a set of notes into an active learning resource rather than a dead collection of information. After several days, not much of that original thinking will be available to them.

8   **Get students note-making together.** Encourage them to work together in small groups, informally, improving their notes by adding things that others in the group have thought of or included. Whether the notes are made from lectures or from source materials, a small syndicate can make a much more useful set of notes than an individual.

9   **Warn students of the danger of thinking, 'I've got the handout, that's all I'll need to take away.'** Remind students that it's not enough just to have captured the information. For example, when a handout is given out in a lecture, many students switch off, because they believe that they already 'have' the lecture. They would be much better advised to edit the handout and make additions to it throughout the lecture, and revisit it within a day or two afterwards.

10   **Help students to realise that summarising is an activity leading to high learning pay-off.** Advise them of the benefits of continually 'distilling' the information they collect – for example, onto small summary cards. This can help them to whittle down large amounts of miscellaneous information

to manageable proportions, helping them make easier work of revision for exams.

11   **Remind students to take care of their notes.** Suggest they should not 'put them all into one basket'. There are many horror stories around of students whose one set of notes was lost or destroyed (or even stolen) at a crucial stage just before their exams. It can be useful to keep summaries in a different place from the original materials, and so on.

25

Helping students to write essays

Despite the fact that in many disciplines, essay-writing counts significantly in the assessment of students (whether in exams or as part of coursework assessment), students are often left to pick up the necessary skills by trial and error. They can be helped to deliver better essays by spending a little time working out where the 'goalposts' are.

1 **Explain that it's worth students' while to become skilled at writing essays.** Highlight the benefits to students. Many forms of assessment involve written communications skills. Furthermore, becoming *faster* at planning and writing essays helps students to make better use of their limited time, and allows them to divert more time to the crucial processes of consolidating their learning and revising for exams.

2 **Encourage students to make essay plans rather than starting 'cold'.** Making a plan can save a lot of time in the long run. When a plan has been made, it is possible to reflect on it for a while, improving the order and coherence of the essay in due course. Remind students that structure is often every bit as important as content.

3 **Bring to students' attention the importance of a good introduction.** The first paragraph or two can set the reader's expectations. This in turn can have a marked bearing on the grade or score that the essay earns. There is no second chance to make a good first impression.

4 **Remind students that a paragraph should essentially be something containing a single idea.** Breaking the essay into good paragraphs helps set out the unfolding ideas, and makes it much easier for the reader to follow arguments and discussions. Many people (including assessors) skim-read, by reading the first (and maybe last) sentence of each paragraph; it is useful for students to bear this in mind.

5   **Stress the importance of a good conclusion.** In assessed essays, this is
likely to be the last part to be read before assessors decide on a grade or
score. Therefore, the better the quality of the finish, the higher may be the
score. Remind students how important it is, therefore, that the conclusions
focus firmly on the question or task as it was set.

6   **Help students understand the criteria used in assessing essays in
their particular subjects.** What counts varies from one discipline to the
next, and often from one assessor to another. Suggest to students that they
should do everything they can to research what different assessors are really
looking for in essays – and respond accordingly when they write. Give your
students some essay titles, then share with them the sort of criteria you
yourself would be looking for in good essays.

7   **Let students try their hands at assessing essays themselves.** Give
them some specimen essays – for example, a good one, a poor one and an
intermediate one. Ask students to analyse them in terms of virtues and faults.
This works best when students can subsequently work in small groups,
comparing their lists of virtues and faults, and generating a prioritised list of
both.

8   **Make it easy for students to generate assessment criteria for essays.**
This can be done using specimen essays, or using essay titles. Ask students
to work out individually (say) 'six important things that should be in an essay
on . . . ', and then have them discuss their criteria with others. It can be useful
to move on from this to getting students to peer-assess each other's written
work, even if doing so is only used as a formative process.

9   **Help students make best use of their time.** It is possible to make several
essay plans in the time that it takes to create one fully fledged essay. The
thinking and learning that occurs in making several essay plans is, however,
much greater than is needed simply to create one finished essay. It is therefore useful to facilitate a session where students generate a series of essay
plans, then assess their plans using criteria they devise themselves.

10   **Help students to make the most of improving their own work.** Advise
students to prepare coursework essays in good time, so that they can put
them out of sight for a few days, then come back to them with fresh eyes.
With creative writing, subconscious thought processes go on continuously,
and the benefits are lost if there is no opportunity to capture second thoughts
and considered views, and use these to improve their work.

26

Helping students to write reports

The nature and style of report-writing vary considerably from one discipline to another. Also, the expectations vary from one tutor to another. There are, however, some general ways that tutors can help students avoid some of the common dangers associated with report-writing.

1   **Help students to find out that there are different kinds of report.** Let them see examples of a variety of formats, and discuss with them the nature of particular report formats for different purposes. Help them to work out what kinds of report are fit for purpose for different contexts; help them to develop the skills they may need for writing research reports in due course.

2   **Advise students to start writing reports early rather than later.** For example, after completing some practical work, it is much easier to write the report when the work is fresh in their memories.

3   **Point out to students the danger of accumulating a backlog of report-writing.** If they have several reports awaiting completion, it is not unusual for the details of the separate pieces of work to begin to merge.

4   **Help students to keep report-writing in perspective.** One of the most serious dangers of leaving report-writing till too late is that students often find themselves catching up with their report-writing while more strategic colleagues have moved on to revision for forthcoming exams.

5   **Encourage students to master word-processing software.** Where students are going to be doing a lot of report-writing, it is worth encouraging them to acquire skills at using an appropriate desktop publishing or word-processing package. Using such tools may be slow at first, but continued practice leads to the ability to produce professional-looking work, and (more importantly) makes it much easier to edit and adjust their work as it nears

completion. The same skills are of course useful for writing essays, CVs, letters of application, and so on.

6 **Titles matter!** Remind students to pay particular attention to choosing a suitable title for each report. Titles become clumsy if they are too long; a short title with additional explanation as a sub-title can be more effective than a long title.

7 **Encourage students to make the rationale of each report clear and understandable.** Remind them to make the aims clear and concise, near the beginning of the report. Then stress how important it is to check that the finished report actually lives up to these aims, and delivers what is promised.

8 **Abstracts are vital.** Most types of report contain a summary or abstract near the beginning. Remind students how important this part is, and suggest that they write it last, when they already know exactly what the conclusions of the work were, and how the report has been structured. This helps to guarantee that the report will 'live up to the promise of its beginning'. It is useful to get students well practised at composing abstracts – for example, by giving them published reports with the abstracts deleted and asking them to compose suitable abstracts, then compare them to each other's efforts and see what works best.

9 **Discuss with students when to use appendices.** For example, detailed descriptions of experimental procedure, or tables of data, and other illustrative material are sometimes best presented as appendices so as not to interrupt the main flow of the discussion in a report.

10 **Help students to develop the main body of their reports.** Explain the importance of discussion and interpretation of data, measurements and observations. Encourage students to give alternative hypotheses when interpretation is inconclusive, and to suggest ways that the investigation could be improved if further work were to be undertaken.

11 **Encourage students to end their reports with a flourish.** It is worth advising students, even when the main findings of a report have been summarised in an abstract or summary at the start of the report, to present the main conclusions at the end as well. These should reflect the aims of the investigation stated at the outset of the report. A good report needs to come to a firm conclusion – it should not just stop!

27

Helping students to learn in laboratories

In many practical subjects, students spend a considerable proportion of their time in laboratories of one kind or another. Laboratory work is essentially hands-on, 'learning-by-doing' work. However, students can benefit from some help in ensuring that they get the most from this kind of learning. Here are some ways you can help them.

1 **Help students to get started straight away.** Do everything you can to avoid wasted time at the start of laboratory sessions. Ensure that technical staff know exactly what will be required well in advance, and that they have the opportunity to have it all set up in time. Also, make sure that students know exactly what they should be doing in each session, and where to go to find what they need to get under way.

2 **Brief students in advance.** Avoid students having to 'tune in' at the start of sessions – for example, having to read a detailed set of instructions before beginning to use some equipment. It is useful to issue such instructions (say) a week in advance, so that students can start their practical work as soon as the session commences.

3 **Make the rationale clear.** Students often don't seem to know why they are doing practical work. Make the links between theory and practical work as clear as possible. Formulate intended learning outcomes for each piece of practical work, so that students know exactly why they're doing it and how it fits into the bigger picture of their programme or module.

4 **Consider structuring students' data-handling.** Where it is necessary for students to write down instrument readings and other quantitative data (and observations), it can be useful to develop a structured worksheet so that students have a clear frame of reference in which to carry out their work. Providing such structured 'skeletons' can be good training for later practical work, when students need to take full responsibility for organising their data-recording themselves.

5   **Help students to make sense of what they're doing.** Try to avoid a situation in which students undertake practical work as if they were merely 'following recipes'. Asking them to interpret what they observe can help to keep their attention on the meaning of what they see and measure.

6   **Avoid log-jams as far as possible.** With large practical classes, try to avoid queuing situations where several students are waiting for a particular piece of equipment to become available. It can be useful to have several different pieces of practical work going on at once, rather than all of the group trying to do the same thing.

7   **Anticipate 'frequently needed help'.** When you identify something you keep having to demonstrate to students, consider ways of preparing a learning resource that can do this for you. A simple, clear set of step-by-step instructions may be all that is needed, or perhaps it's worth making a video or a computer-based demonstration so that your help is packaged up in a way that is available to anyone at any time.

8   **Be quite firm about report deadlines.** Remind students that the sooner they write a report, the less time it actually takes, as they remember better what they actually did! One of the most significant dangers of practical work is that students can accumulate a backlog in their report-writing. This can lead them to be catching up on reports when they should have been pre-paring for exams, and often leads to exam failure. Instituting a fairly strict regime regarding report submission will be useful to your students, especially if you explain exactly why you are doing so.

9   **Let them know how much it counts.** Make it clear to your students how much the laboratory work contributes to their overall assessment. This allows them to judge how much time and energy they should be spending on such work.

10 **Help your students to develop relevant research skills.** Encourage them to *try to make sense* of what they observe and measure, and not just report their findings without thinking deeply about what they mean. When devising assessment criteria for laboratory work, make sure that important skills such as interpretation, imagination and initiative are included appropriately in the assessment criteria.

28

Helping students to plan their projects

In many programmes (particularly in the final year of degree programmes), students undertake project work that makes a significant contribution to their overall assessment profile. This work may take up a substantial amount of their time. Spending a little time helping students plan the way they will handle large tasks such as projects, can help them deliver much better results.

1   **Help them to work out exactly what they are trying to achieve.** Encourage students to take some time working out the overall aim of their project. The aims – or intended project outcomes – should address questions such as 'Why is this project important?' and 'What is the project aiming to achieve?'

2   **Help students to break down large tasks into manageable chunks.** Suggest to students that they should break down the overall aim into a series of steps through which the aim can be achieved. Each of these steps can then be phrased as an objective or intended outcome, helping to create a definite and tangible frame of reference around which to plan work on the project.

3   **Help students to take ownership of the processes involved.** Suggest that they look at each of the objectives or outcomes they've worked out, asking, 'How best can this one be achieved?' This enables them to map out the range of processes they will need to use as they carry out the research, fieldwork or practical work involved.

4   **Make it possible for students to gain early feedback on their plans.** Once they have worked out an overall aim, a series of intended outcomes, and a summary of the processes to be used to achieve the objectives, it's worth their turning these into a draft outline of the proposed project, so that feedback can be sought at this early stage. A one-page outline can be the basis for valuable feedback from tutors, fellow students, supervisors,

and so on. Early feedback can help students avoid the risk of floundering unsuccessfully for some time, reducing the time and energy remaining to them to get to grips with their projects.

5 **Help students to structure collaborative work.** Where projects are going to be developed by students in groups, advise them to plan out at this stage the respective contributions individuals are going to make to the overall product. It can be useful for the groups to do an informal 'strengths, weaknesses, opportunities, threats' analysis, so that each of them contributes in the most productive manner.

6 **Help students to plan 'who does what' in collaborative work.** Where students are developing projects in groups, it is useful to get them to add to the emerging action plan precise details of 'what is going to be done by whom, starting when and finishing when?'. This can be turned into a visual form by making a chart with time running horizontally and tasks vertically, drawing 'bars' across the chart showing the duration of each task, and writing on the bars the name of the student who will be working on that task.

7 **Advise students to turn the project proposals into an action plan.** This can be done by building timescales and stage deadlines into their plans. In many circumstances it is useful to advise them to set a completion deadline using only half of the available time. This allows time for reflection and development, and for the production of a better final project. It also builds in leeway to handle things that may go wrong, or measurements that may have to be repeated.

8 **Advise students on how best to present their work.** Before they start work on the respective tasks, it is useful for students to start thinking about the format they will use to report their findings. Formats may include written reports, oral presentations or a combination of both. Reports may be in a highly specified form, or there may be a great deal of freedom. Suggest that students work out exactly how the results of each of the tasks in their action plans will contribute to the final reporting process.

9 **Get students to build self-assessment into their work.** A highly productive way of helping students to deliver projects of good quality is to help them start thinking about what the assessment criteria are likely to be. Often it is possible to ask the students themselves to present a suggested framework of assessment criteria. They can then receive feedback regarding the appropriateness of the criteria they have worked out. When students undertake project work against a clear background of the assessment criteria, their chances of achieving the criteria are maximised.

10 **Help students to make the most of the people around them.** Lecturers and tutors (and other people) can be very useful 'expert witnesses' during the ongoing work of a project. Encourage students to work out whom they can use in such a capacity, and how best to go about it.

29

Getting feedback from your students

Feedback is a vital process in any kind of learning. Not least, we need feedback to develop positive feelings about what we do as tutors (and of course to find out about things we may not yet be doing well enough). The following are just some ways you can gather feedback from your students – and thereby help to adjust what you do to help them to learn more successfully.

1   **Watch their faces.** There's a wealth of information to be gained from the body language of students in large groups, in small groups and individually. Facial expressions will often tell you things that they would not put into words.

2   **Watch their backs!** You may not be able to do this yourself, but a colleague can help you here. In a large group it's useful to have someone 'watching from behind' now and then. You may be able to learn of things going on that you had no idea about.

3   **Open up dialogue possibilities.** 'Are there any parts you'd like me to say a bit more about?' is a useful question. It's better than 'Are there parts you don't understand?' or 'Any questions?' Seeking out which parts 'didn't get across first time' leads to useful feedback in its own right. Sometimes it's easier to get such feedback in one-to-one chats or in tutorials than in a large group.

4   **Now and then, give out a short questionnaire.** For example, provide your students with some alternative 'feelings words' to ring or underline. Possibilities include 'bored', 'interested', 'enthused', 'puzzled', 'stimulated', 'irritated', 'tired', 'swamped', 'intimidated', 'lulled to sleep', 'condescended to', and so on. Don't take offence at the negative words they may choose; regard all feedback as potentially useful information.

5   **Find out what they think about how their learning is going.** When your students have covered several topics, give them a list of what they've done, with three columns for them to tick regarding how well they believe they have got their heads round each topic. Column headings such as 'no problems with this', 'just about fine with this' and 'not yet able to do this' can be useful. This sort of feedback gives you useful information about what got across and what didn't.

6   **Help them to revisit the intended learning outcomes.** This is another way of finding out how they think they're getting on. Give them a list of the learning outcomes (if necessary translated into student-friendly language). Provide three columns for them to choose from, such as 'I've completely achieved this', 'I've partly achieved this', 'I'm nowhere near achieving this yet', and ask them to rate how they feel about each outcome at this particular stage in their learning.

7   **Occasionally give out open-ended free-response questionnaires.** For example, ask students (anonymously) to write down answers to 'the two things I most like about the programme are . . . and the two things I like least about the programme are . . . '. It's possible to get some quite hurtful replies to the latter – but all feedback is useful if you accept it in the right spirit.

8   **Sometimes seek feedback from groups rather than individuals.** Asking a group to give opinions gives students the chance to compare their views, and spares individuals being associated with particularly strong views – it can feel more anonymous coming from a group than from an individual. Getting a group to fill in a questionnaire can be a useful and interesting experience. Where there is disagreement in how members of the group feel about a particular question, they will often elaborate on the questionnaire (such as 'three of us liked this, two of us didn't'). The things that cause mixed feelings may be an important area of feedback for you.

9   **Seek feedback from individuals you happen to have occasion to talk to.** With a large class, you may have detailed discussions with any particular student only now and again, but you can still get useful feedback information from such occasions if you search for it. 'Which bit are you finding best, and why?' may sometimes be a better question than just 'How's it going, then?'

10 **Make the most of feedback from colleagues.** This can be especially productive in team-teaching situations. The main reason why professional people don't give each other enough feedback is that they don't ask each other directly for it. You can break this chain. Many of your colleagues will have a fairly good idea about how *your* teaching is going; they pick up signals from students all the time. These colleagues may be reluctant to volunteer the feedback to you, but when asked, they will usually tell you – at least about the 'good news'.

Chapter 4

Helping students to learn from resources

Our suggestions here are connected both with learning resources you may design for your students, and with other facilities that may be available for them to use – not least, the library.

30

Designing learning resources

Increasing use is being made of resource-based learning as part of the processes used by students on college-based programmes. Some resources may be entirely print based – for example, interactive handouts including tasks and feedback responses. Others may be computer based, or available online. The following guidelines may help you design effective learning resources for your own students.

1   **Make the intended learning outcomes abundantly clear.** Choose the wording so as to help students to *want* to achieve the intended outcomes. Help them to see *why* they need to work towards achieving them: let them know how important each of the main outcomes is in the overall picture. Make it easy for *them* to tell when they have achieved each outcome.

2   **Build in plenty of activity.** Learning happens by having a go, trial and error, practice and repetition. Compose structured self-assessment questions and activities based on each of the learning outcomes. Pay particular attention to the wording of these questions and activities, so that students working alone will interpret them as intended.

3   **Compensate for the fact that students may be studying on their own.** They've only got information on paper and/or on screen, without the benefits of your tone of voice, body language, emphasis, and so on. Therefore, it is vital that the learning resource materials are as unambiguous as possible, so that students always know exactly what they're supposed to be doing with them.

4   **Make sure that students get feedback all the time, not just when they've finished using the learning resource material.** For each self-assessment question, design a feedback response that does more than simply provide students with the answer to the question. Students need to find out the answers to their questions 'was I right?' and 'If not, why not?'

5 **Build in open-ended tasks as well as structured tasks.** Then provide some guidelines to allow students to judge for themselves the extent to which they have tackled the tasks successfully. Keep channels of communication open, so that they can ask you about anything they're still not sure about.

6 **Build in tutor-marked assignments or exercises.** These allow you to check that students' learning is proceeding well, and to find out which students may need additional help (or pressure!) to keep them learning successfully from the resource materials. Furthermore, students' work on such assignments helps you to see where the problems in the materials themselves may be, and therefore how best to edit and improve the materials.

7 **Test your resource materials out with live students.** It is really useful when developing new materials to be able to watch students using them for the first time. Observe their progress with the self-assessment questions and activities. See where they work through the materials without any problems, and, more importantly, watch for where they get stuck.

8 **Seek feedback on the resource materials.** Ask students whether they made any mistakes that weren't responded to by the feedback responses. Ask them whether there were any places where the materials were going 'too fast' (or too slowly) for them. Ask them what they enjoyed most about the materials – and what they didn't like at all.

9 **Try the materials out on colleagues too.** Try to persuade them not just to look at the materials, but to work quickly through the tasks and activities. They will often be able to give you really useful feedback about potential problems in the materials, and may be able to alert you to anything that is 'wrong' with the subject matter.

31

Helping students to use resource-based learning materials

For some students, learning on their own, using resources, is something new. A little help regarding how best to go about handling resource-based learning materials can help students maximise the benefits to them of being able to work at their own pace, at times of their own choosing, and in their own styles.

1 **Enthuse your students with the benefits of working on their own.** Remind them particularly of the freedom to learn at their own pace, in places of their own choosing, and at times that suit them.

2 **Warn your students that it's up to them!** Point out that with the resource-based learning elements of their programmes or modules, there will be no one looking over their shoulder to make sure that they're getting down to it. It is also up to them to find out whether there are any problems they need help with, and, if there are, to approach tutors or others to help them to sort out such problems.

3 **Point out to your students the value of learning outcomes.** Show them how to use these as a means of mapping their progress and keeping track of how their learning is going. Also point out that, sooner or later, their achievement of these learning outcomes will be assessed in one way or another, along with all the other elements of their studying.

4 **Encourage students to keep active.** Remind your students that most learning is 'by doing'. Point out that the activities, tasks and self-assessment questions in resource-based learning – whether online or on paper – are the 'doing' opportunities, and that if they are skipped, not much real learning can happen.

5 **Help your students to make the most of feedback while they learn from resources.** Point out that in well-designed learning resource materials,

much of this feedback tends to come from 'responses' to tasks, choices, activities and self-assessment questions. Remind them that such feedback will be of real value to them only *after* they've had a try at the questions and activities (in other words, in print-based materials, for example, looking too early at the answers will rob them of valuable learning opportunities).

6   **Guide your students about what's really important and what's simply background.** Help them establish what they 'need to know', as against what is merely 'nice to know'. A quick way of doing this is to star-rate the intended learning outcomes in the materials. Or, where the outcomes are not pre-sented explicitly in the materials themselves, issue your students with a list of the intended outcomes to help them see exactly what they should be gaining as they use the materials.

7   **Check that students know exactly what to do with the illustrations in the materials.** This particularly applies to diagrams, graphs, tables, charts, and so on. The biggest problem with many learning resource materials is the uncertainty students feel regarding 'what am I expected to do with this?'. For example, in the case of a table of data, have they to learn it, or interpret it, or spot a trend, or something else? A few words of guidance regarding each illustration can prevent students wasting energy on things they need not learn.

8   **Make sure that there are sufficient opportunities for revision, reflec-tion and consolidation.** A problem with learning resource materials is that they may cover something well, but only once – and then assume it's been mastered by students. Add on revision exercises or tutor-marked assignments to help students retain important skills and knowledge.

9   **Point out the advantages of *not* working alone when learning from resource materials.** Encourage students to take advantage of any oppor-tunities they get to work with a few colleagues. Show them how quickly they can break down assumptions they may have made. Remind them how useful it is to explain something to someone else.

10   **Prepare your own study guide to resource-based learning elements.** This is worth doing if the materials are bought in; even if you wrote the materials yourself. A study guide can be updated much more quickly than original materials, and can respond quickly to the problems you will be alerted to through feedback from your students. It's useful to build up a list of 'frequently asked questions' arising from students' experience of using the particular materials involved. Also, ensure that there are effective safety mechanisms for students who go off the rails or fall too far behind. Make sure they know where to go for help, who can help them, and when is the best time to seek help.

32

Using moving images to help learning

Videos, DVDs and streamed video from the Internet are in everyday use in teaching, particularly in well-equipped lecture theatres. However, because there are television sets and video and DVD players in most homes and public places, attitudes to what is seen on-screen have changed, and people don't tend to take much notice of most of what is seen on the small screen. For educational video to work, therefore, we need to look again at exactly why we're using it, and what the students are intended to get out of it. The following suggestions may help you to put moving images to work in your students' learning.

1   **Decide exactly why you're going to use moving images.** While it is perfectly acceptable to use a video extract as a break in a lecture, or as icing on the cake, or even purely for entertainment, it is important that students know which use is intended.

2   **Think about the intended learning outcomes.** When you are using moving images with your students, work out exactly what you intend them to be able to do, after seeing the sequence, that they may not have been able to do already. It's useful to give students these intended learning outcomes in advance, so they know (even subconsciously) what to take particular notice of as they view the video.

3   **Remember that concentration spans are short.** Students sitting quite still in a comfortable room looking for more than a short while at moving images on a screen are likely to go to sleep! A few well-chosen clips may be better than a 30-minute documentary or debate – however interesting it is.

4   **When possible, get students to create an agenda before watching a video extract.** If they have previously thought of questions they want answered, or identified things they wish to look out for, they have at least some ownership of what they are watching, rather than simply being bombarded with audio-visual information.

5   **Analyse your reasons for wishing to use moving images.** For example, video is particularly useful for showing not only things in motion, but also facial expression, body language, interpersonal behaviour, and so on. Moving images can also give students an impression of things they would not otherwise be able to see, such as industrial processes, distant geological features, time-lapse sequences, microscope details, and so on. Share your reasons for choosing to use video with your students.

6   **Keep things simple.** It's fairly straightforward to build links into video sequences in your PowerPoint™ files, and this can be much less hassle than having to switch systems in a lecture theatre if you're already using data projection. However, check that the projected quality is going to be adequate.

7   **Remember that with on-screen images being such a common part of everyday life, we forget much of what we see on-screen.** Find ways of 'capturing' the important things. For example, pause now and then to pose a question or two to the group of students, or to get them discussing the implications of something they have just seen.

8   **Help the important things to get into students' notes.** Where important conclusions are to be drawn from viewing a screen, find ways in which the conclusions can be transferred to paper. A short supporting handout can be enough to remind students of things they were shown on the screen. Alternatively, give students a few minutes now and then to jot down their own conclusions or reactions to what they have just seen.

9   **Make sure that students know when there's an assessment-related agenda.** Where learning outcomes derived from moving images materials are important enough to have assessment criteria directly associated with them, make sure that students are aware of the situation. For example, if exam questions will require students to use information they have gathered from moving images, it is important that students are alerted to this in advance, so that their viewing will be sufficiently active.

10 **Think about group size.** Work out whether it is best to use moving images with large groups of students (for example, projected onto the large screen in a lecture theatre, providing a 'shared experience' for the whole group) or with smaller tutorial groups (where detailed discussion is more easily possible).

11 **Play it again?** Where possible, arrange that a copy of each video can be viewed again by students (for example, students who may have missed the original screening, or who want to look again in more depth). Small video files are easily placed onto intranets so that students can return to them when they wish.

33

Helping students to learn online

Virtual learning environments, computer conferencing systems and email are widely available to students in educational institutions. The following suggestions may help your students to make the most of such media.

1   **Give students something to do to get them started.** Most students are very familiar with virtual learning environments and email long before they reach higher education, but there will be some who are not (sometimes mature students). Just playing with the systems isn't enough to get everyone into using them, so it's worth having some identified search tasks using the Internet to get everyone into it, and some required online tasks so that you can find out whether there are any students who need a little extra help.

2   **Keep reminding students about the associated intended learning outcomes.** Students need to know exactly what they're supposed to be getting out of online tasks, and how this learning integrates with all the other parts of their learning on a programme or module. When students know exactly what they're intended to do, there's much more chance that they will do it!

3   **Remind students to save things.** Whenever students are working online or using computers in any other circumstances, the worst thing that happens is that they may lose their work through not having saved it frequently (or not knowing where they've saved it to!). Persuade students to make back-up copies of their own work, and to label floppy disks or CDs so they don't lose track of where they've saved things.

4   **Build online work into the normal fabric of students' learning.** If they see that the work they do online is a natural part of the bigger picture, they take it more seriously and are less likely to be led astray by the attractions of just playing with the Internet.

5   **Get students to help each other.** Students are very good at showing each other how to work with all the new advances of technology. Don't forget that explaining how to do something is useful for the explainer as well as the recipient. The acts of explaining and guiding are useful learning experiences in themselves.

6   **Alert students to the danger of just drifting.** It's easy to get mouse-happy and just click along through online or computer-based learning pathways without any real learning happening. Suggest to students that they need to be making some kind of notes as they go along – something that will capture what they are learning in a form whereby it can be used as a reminder.

7   **'Now you see it, now it's gone!'** This can be the greatest problem for anyone working online or with computer-based learning materials. Some really important information may be up on screen one minute, but at the next click of the mouse it may be gone – and not always easy to get back to. Help students to become better at deciding what they really need to capture from each screen they view – or at least making good decisions about what they don't need to capture.

8   **Consider putting some assessed work online.** With the 'Track Changes' feature of Microsoft Word (for example), you can give tutor feedback to individual students by marking up suggested changes in their writing, or adding comments of your own. It can be considerably quicker to return their 'marked' work online in this way than to write comments by hand on paper, and you can easily save a record of your marked-up files so that you remember what comments you have made to which students.

9   **Consider using virtual learning environments to include an 'agony column' for your programme or module.** Encourage students to enter their problems and to reply to each other's problems. Reply to important issues yourself, as expert witness, when appropriate.

10 **Remind students of 'netiquette' expectations.** Agree on some ground rules for computer conferencing entries. For example, language should not be obscene, entries should not put anyone down, sexism and racism should be strictly avoided, and so on. Many institutions have severe penalties for anyone found to have abused the system.

34

Helping students to use the library or learning resource centre

When they first go to a new institution, students normally have some sort of library tour, or even some library training. However, like anything else, if it's not quickly followed up by being put into practice, much of it is forgotten.

1 **Help students to take ownership of becoming really skilled at information tracking and retrieval.** Help students to see how useful it will be to them in the long run to become efficient at tracking down resources in the library or learning resources centre. This will save them from wasting a considerable amount of time – often at stages in their studies when time is particularly precious.

2 **Remind students that a library is more than just a computer terminal.** Some students seem to think that a terminal with Internet access is all they need for studying. Campus-based libraries invariably have just such terminals, but also contain all the text-based resources: books, journals, magazines, and so on.

3 **Remind students of the benefits of printed resources.** In this age of computer-based resources and online information, students sometimes miss out on the fact that when using a textbook or journal it's easier to find one's way backwards and forwards than when working online. It can be easier to know 'where one is' with a book, and to flick pages backwards and forwards until the most relevant part is found.

4 **Give students some things to do in the library.** Build in such tasks really early in the programme, so that students don't end up putting off the moment of finding out all about the library until they're too busy to have time to do it well. Set tasks (for example, preparations for tutorials) that require students to track down particular reference materials. Plan the tasks so that they

become experienced at using the search facilities for both textbooks and journals, and then gain speed in physically locating the materials.

5 **Help students to know where to check regularly.** Give them tasks or exercises that get them familiar with where the most relevant stock is housed and where the new journals will be shelved, and the back-issues of the important ones. It can be useful to help them to find out where the stock on study skills is housed, too, so they can use the library not only to find out what to study, but also how best to go about being a successful student.

6 **Consider giving students both collaborative and private tasks to do in the library.** For example, set a group task to identify source materials on a given topic, but then an individual task to produce an annotated bibliography on (say) ten of the sources they find. The group stage can help students to help each other find their way around the resources, and the individual stage can make sure that students don't take their collaboration too far and allow passengers to benefit too much from the work of their more diligent colleagues.

7 **Help students to make the most of the human resources in the library.** Remind students that library staff are usually very willing to offer help and advice, particularly when not simply being asked to do routine tasks such as finding a particular book. Often, subject librarians not only will have a detailed knowledge of the relevant stock in their subject, but also will have a good understanding of the subject itself, and be able to advise on which books and references are particularly worthwhile.

8 **Get students up to speed at making reference to published work.** Train students in the correct way to refer to source materials. Lead by example, and take as much care with your citing and referencing in your handouts for students as you would need to take to get your work accepted for publication by a pernickety journal editor! It can be useful to give your students a prize quiz – for example, a list of 100 sources in the library containing ten 'mistakes' – and offer the prize to the student who finds the ten mistakes first!

9 **Encourage students to use their eyes!** For example, when there are several copies of a book on the shelves (or on the computer catalogue listing), it is probable that the book is more useful than when only a single copy exists. Also, well-worn books (especially recent yet well-work books) have obviously proved more useful than 'pristine' books.

10 **Help your students to find out whether the library is a good place for them to settle down to study.** Some students find that they work best in places such as libraries, away from other distractions. Ensure that your students know of the availability of study spaces (and carrels) and know the

opening times of libraries. Encourage them to try out late evenings and weekends, when there may be more space to spread out books and papers, and easier access to stock.

11 **Help students to make the most of the non-text resources in the library or learning resources centre.** Most such facilities have shelves of videos, DVDs, CDs and other electronic recording formats that can be accessed for student learning, including legal archives, image libraries, and so on, which can be integral to students' independent learning.

35

Helping students to learn from handouts

The use of handout materials has increased, and even more material is often made available to students online to edit up and print out themselves. However, the danger remains that handouts can be just information, and may be safely filed away instead of being processed by students turning the information into their own knowledge. The following suggestions may help your students get more from your handouts, and may make your own time preparing handouts better spent.

1   **Make handouts look attractive.** The quality of the message is now inextricably associated with the quality of the medium; scrappy handouts tend not to be valued by students.

2   **Help your students to find their way easily around your handouts.** Use plenty of headings and sub-headings. There's little more off-putting than a solid page of unbroken text. It can be useful to use question headings so that students can tell at a glance exactly what the next paragraph or two of the handout are about. When a glance at a handout gives information about the structure of its contents, it has already started to help people learn.

3   **Use white space.** For students to develop a sense of ownership of handouts, they need to have room to write their own notes onto them. Space between paragraphs, space at the top and bottom of pages, or a wide margin on one side are all ways of giving them this possibility of ownership. Students take more care of handouts they've added to – they're less likely to end their days as paper aeroplanes!

4   **Let students know what they should be getting out of the handout.** Use the start of a handout to remind students what its purposes are. It can be useful to head each handout with a statement of the particular intended learning outcomes directly associated with it.

5   **Build learning by doing into your handouts.** Don't just give students information; give them some tasks or exercises to get them processing the information. Consider some things for them to do straight away – for example, during the lecture or tutorial that the handout may accompany. Also consider adding things for them to do as follow-up tasks – for example, using textbooks and journal articles.

6   **Include boxes for students to do things in handouts.** Structured tasks are best, such as 'think of six reasons why the economy is in recession and list them below'. The fact that space has been provided for students' answers helps persuade them (often subconsciously) to have a try at the tasks rather than simply skip them, and asking for an identified number of points gets them thinking of the *other* factors that may not be quite so easy to think of as the first two or three that come to mind.

7   **Give students the chance to learn from their mistakes.** Multiple-choice questions can be useful for this. The handout can serve as a useful reminder of wrong options chosen, as well as a pleasant reminder of correct (or best) choices. A pre-lecture and/or post-lecture quiz in multiple-choice format can be a useful way of alerting students to what they should be getting their heads around during the lecture.

8   **Use handouts to save students the drudgery of just copying down things they see or hear in class.** Copying things down is a low-level learning activity. Having such information already in handout form allows you to spend face-to-face time probing into the meaning of the information: interpreting it, questioning it, extrapolating from it, analysing it, and so on.

9   **Consider issuing handouts in advance of sessions.** One way of doing this is to make them available online a week or so before the scheduled session, and to ask students to bring their copies with them to the session. Think about adding one or two short 'pre-class tasks' to such handouts, and you can then get at least some of the students thinking about the agenda before the class, and can spend the first few minutes checking out with the group how well they got on with the tasks. There are implications here concerning printing costs however.

10 **Build some group tasks into your handouts.** For example, during a lecture or tutorial you can plan some tasks in which students brainstorm ideas or discuss case-study data with their neighbours, and enter their thoughts or conclusions into boxes already provided on the handout. This helps students not only to learn with each other more actively during the session, but also to retain what they're learned in this way.

11 **Store your handouts on disk.** Next time you run a class on the same topic, it can be far quicker to edit and improve an existing handout than to write a new one from scratch. If you use lots of handouts, you'll need to take care that your file names and folders are sufficiently clear for you to be able to locate the right handout quickly next time round. It can be useful to include 'date of use' in the file name.

Chapter 5

Assessment: demonstrating evidence of achievement

Our emphasis here is on ways of letting students in on the 'secrets' of assessment criteria, and developing self-assessment and peer assessment as ways of deepening the quality of their learning. We also include some suggestions for helping students cope with more traditional forms of assessment.

36

Helping students to see the big picture

1   **Remember how important assessment is in practice.** 'Students can escape from bad teaching, but they can't escape from bad assessment' (David Boud, 1995). Assessing students' work is the most important thing that their tutors may do for them – if we get it wrong, it can affect students' entire careers.

2   **Accept that assessment drives students' learning.** Most students are quite strategic in that they only really put a lot of energy into learning something if it counts towards their overall assessment. We can do a lot to help them to turn this into a useful driving force, helping them where it is most important for them to spend their time and energy.

3   **Remember that students can be too close to assessment to see how it all works objectively.** For example, if they are revising earnestly for forthcoming exams, they can lose sight of what would be reasonable questions as they simply try to retain everything they have learned (or catch up with everything they feel they should have learned).

4   **Remind students that in some ways it's all a game.** Remind them also that the rules of the game are designed by those who design the assessed tasks or set the exam questions, and by those who actually do the assessing in due course. In other words, students need to do everything they can to tune in to the assessment culture around them – other people's culture – and need to become expert in how it all works as well as learning what's expected of them in their subject matter.

5   **Alert students to how much they can learn from – and with – each other.** Although at the end of the day, assessment may seem to be a competitive business, they can become much better equipped to play the game if they talk to each other about it along the way. In particular, they can learn a great deal about how assessment works by getting into peer

assessment and self-assessment, rather than just waiting for examiners to assess their work.

6   **Link intended learning outcomes clearly to assessment.** Ideally, students should be assessed quite directly and overtly on their achievement of the intended learning outcomes. When this is done, the learning outcomes themselves can be very useful to students as they prepare for assessment, as they can self-assess the level of their achievement along the way and adjust their efforts so that they can demonstrate their achievement fully when required.

7   **Remind students that we actually assess *evidence* of their achievement.** In other words, we can't directly assess 'what students know' or 'what they understand' other than by getting them to *demonstrate* what they know or understand. Sometimes this evidence will be in written forms, such as essays or exam answers. At other times the evidence will be oral in nature, as in oral exams or interviews.

8   **Help students to work out the standards.** There are several ways of helping students to tune in to the expected standards by which their evidence of achievement of the intended learning outcomes will in due course be judged. They can gain an indication of the expected standards from the wording of the intended learning outcomes themselves (if they are clearly written). They can gain further information about standards from the assessment criteria linked to these outcomes. Yet more information about standards can be forthcoming from descriptors of the evidence that students are working towards producing to demonstrate their achievement.

9   **Give students rehearsal opportunities.** Practice makes perfect. Particularly where students are meeting assessment formats for the first time, they need the opportunity to find out (by trial and error where possible, but without penalty) how a new assessment process actually works. They need to become better able to handle each new kind of assessment, and show themselves at their best in each new context.

10 **Alert students to the value of feedback on assessed work.** While they may get precious little feedback on exams (other than scores or grades, or just finding that they have passed or failed), there is a lot of value in the feedback associated with coursework assessment. Help them to realise how useful it can be to look at what went wrong with a low-scoring element of coursework, and to learn from this how to make the next piece of coursework better, and so on.

37

Helping students to set their sights high

Students need to know where the goalposts are. When they are familiar with how assessment actually works, and the nature of the associated assessment criteria, they are better able to perform in ways that they know will meet the criteria. Tutors necessarily develop considerable expertise in assessment, but this expertise is sometimes not shared with the students in ways that would help them to demonstrate their achievement at its best. The following suggestions can help students gain familiarity with – and confidence about – the rules of the game of assessment.

1 **Show students marking schemes.** These can be from examinations or coursework assignments. Then explain exactly how the criteria are applied to typical specimen answers. Help students to see where marks are gained, and particularly address examples of where marks could be lost.

2 **Issue students with marking criteria to apply to their own work.** Give them the opportunity to learn about their strengths and weaknesses by assessing samples of their own work. Act as an expert witness when they are unsure about the interpretation of the marking criteria in the particular context of their own answers.

3 **Issue students with assessment criteria to apply to each other's work.** Encourage them not simply to swap their work with friends, but to continue to exchange work until no one knows who is assessing anyone's piece of work. Act as an expert witness during the peer assessment, helping with the interpretation of the criteria in the light of particular students' answers.

4 **Get students to brainstorm a set of assessment criteria themselves.** It can be useful to do this for a particular piece of work they have just done, or – better still – are about to do. Alternatively, take in examples of work done by previous students and get students to devise criteria based on good and bad examples of past work. Help them rephrase each of the criteria into

words that they can apply with a minimum of uncertainty. Ask them to give relative weights to each of the criteria (for example, by asking them to apportion 30 marks among eight criteria) and then in due course arrange for them to apply their criteria to their own or each other's work.

5 **Get students to play examiner.** In a whole-group session such as a lecture slot, show students a past exam question or coursework question and facilitate their production of a set of assessment criteria for the question. Issue to the students (in groups) a selection of good, poor and intermediate specimen answers to the question and allow the students to assess each example. Discuss in plenary the findings, explaining where necessary how particular criteria should have been applied to the respective specimens, and exploring the score or grade each specimen should have been awarded.

6 **Give students feedback about their application of assessment criteria.** For example, where students have self-assessed or peer-assessed their own work, act as a moderator. Collect in the student-marked work and check that the assessment has been done objectively. Write feedback comments as necessary about the quality of assessment, and return these to the students who did the assessing.

7 **Ask students (in groups) to design an examination or coursework assignment for an area they have studied.** Ask them to assign marks to each question and question part. Then ask them to write out a marking sched-ule for their examination or assignment, and where necessary to readjust the questions so that the answers could be more objectively assessed. In plenary, act as expert witness, showing how typical examiners might address the assessment of a selection of the questions the students generated.

8 **Help students to find out what they learn through assessing.** Where students have participated in self-assessment or peer assessment, ask them each to write down things they learned from the experience of applying assessment criteria. Draw from the students a list of their experiences. This normally shows that the act of assessing is in itself a highly productive way of learning about a subject.

9 **Encourage students in groups or pairs to design tasks for each other, and assessment criteria for each task.** Ask the students to carry out the tasks and peer-assess each other's work using the criteria they designed. Ask the students then to explain to each other exactly how the work was assessed. Act as troubleshooter in cases where particular students feel that criteria were unfair, or assessment was not objective.

10 **Help students to see the differences between 'first impression' marking and 'objective' marking.** Give students an example of an

examination answer or coursework assignment answer and ask them to (quickly) give it a 'first impression' mark out of (say) 20, recording their scores. Then guide them through an objective assessment of the sample, and discuss particular differences between the subjective scores and the objective ones. Help them to see the things that led to poor 'first impression' marks, so that they can avoid losing such marks themselves in future.

38

Giving students written feedback

Although we're using the term 'feedback' here, we're referring to helping students find out our answer not just to their question 'how did I do?', but also to their question 'what can I do better next time?' – some call this 'feed-forward'. Written feedback from you can be regarded by students as very authoritative. This has advantages and disadvantages. The following suggestions may help ensure that your feedback is received well by your students, and used well by them to develop their performance in future assessment contexts.

1   **Accept that you may be seen as an authority.** When you're marking students' work, they will be aware that you have already succeeded. You are likely to have already achieved the qualifications they are aiming for – and perhaps much more. Remember that when students receive their work back covered with feedback comments from you, their feelings may be quite heightened. In other words, they can be particularly sensitive to the feedback they receive, especially the first few comments they read.

2   **Numbers count!** Where a score or a grade is given, this can dominate students' reactions. If the score is high, they may be pleased – but may then not go on to read the feedback in any detail. If the score is low, they may be dispirited – and not read the feedback at all! Decide whether the score is important – or whether it would be better to give feedback without a score.

3   **Make the most of remediation.** Remind yourself that the primary purposes of giving students tutor-marked work is to let them find out exactly how they are doing, and what to do about any weak areas.

4   **Don't make your students see red!** Think about the effect red ink has on students. Even when an excellent essay or report is returned covered with red comments (however positive), there is an instinctive anxiety on seeing 'all the red' on the script. This anxiety can get in the way of receiving feedback in a calm, objective way.

5   **Don't cross your students!** Easy as it is to insert crosses (beside errors or wrong answers), crosses can be strongly demotivating to students. Crosses may remind them of unhappy memories of schooldays. It can be better to use words when possible.

6   **Don't tick your students off too much!** It is all too easy to put ticks beside correct answers or ideas, when phrases such as 'good point', 'well done', 'nicely put', 'the hub of your argument' give pleasure to students, along with real feedback.

7   **Help students to see easily exactly what you're giving them feedback about.** For example, consider using a highlighter pen to mark over incorrect phrases or words in scripts, rather than crossing them out or underlining them or ringing them. Margin notes or footnotes can add explanations relating to the highlighted words or phrases, so that students can quickly tell exactly what you're getting at. Another way of adding comments, without defacing students' work, is to stick Post-it™ notes onto their pages, with each explanatory comment bearing a code or number so that it can be linked easily to the point in their work to which it belongs.

8   **Don't let your feedback get squashed.** Where longer feedback comments and explanations are needed, prepare a separate feedback sheet with numbered points referring to identified parts of the marked work. A more structured way of giving detailed feedback is to prepare assignment return sheets listing the assessment criteria, giving these sheets out when setting the assignment, and returning the sheet completed with your comments along with the marked assignment.

9   **Prepare some 'generic' feedback.** Save yourself time, and provide even more feedback, by preparing model answers to questions and assignments, with your own commentary showing typical dangers and key points. You can then link particular comments on individual assignments to the model answers, saving you having to repeatedly write out explanations to common difficulties.

10   **Make a digestible sandwich.** When providing a summary of feedback comments (such as an overall review of a piece of work), try to start *and finish* with something positive. Remember that students' feelings may sink if they see a word as innocuous as 'however' (which is so often followed by 'bad news'), and would plummet with phrases such as 'you've failed to grasp the basics'!

11   **Get at least some feedback to students at the time when they hand in their work.** For feedback to be really effective, it needs to reach students as fast as possible, while their ideas are still fresh in their minds. Since

is impossible to mark a large pile of scripts immediately, one way of compensating for an inevitable delay regarding feedback is to issue model answers and commentaries immediately after students hand in their work for assessment. This gives them immediate generic feedback on the task, and you can then prepare specific individual feedback with less urgency – and do so much more quickly knowing that the generic feedback addressed many of the most frequently needed points.

12   **Consider using some automated feedback.** Explore how your institution supports computer-aided assessment and investigate to what extent you can include an element of automated feedback on written work.

39

Giving face-to-face feedback to students

Giving face-to-face feedback to students has both advantages and disadvantages as compared with giving them written feedback. Here we present some ideas to help students gain maximum benefit from verbal feedback.

1 **Students can be quite tense in your distinguished presence!** Students may see tutors both as experts and as figures of authority. The additional tension this can create can cause them to receive feedback in a somewhat distorted way, sometimes extrapolating beyond reason your actual words and the manner in which you give them feedback.

2 **There's much more to face-to-face feedback than words.** Verbal feedback processes can convey more information than written feedback, since you have tone of voice, facial expression and body language over and above the words you choose to use.

3 **A problem with verbal feedback is that it is transient.** It is not easy for students to reflect accurately on the feedback they receive face to face, as they tend to remember particular parts of it better than others.

4 **Students' moods vary.** The reactions of students to verbal feedback can depend a lot on their state of mind at the time of receiving the feedback. If they are feeling positive and optimistic, they may remember mainly the positive things you say, while if they are feeling apprehensive, they may remember mainly the critical comments you offer.

5 **Make the most of the two-way nature of face-to-face feedback.** An advantage of verbal feedback processes is that they are normally interactive. You can observe what effects the words you use are having, and add further explanations when it is clear that your message is not yet getting across.

6   **Choose wisely how many faces to give feedback to at a time.** Think carefully about whether to give particular sorts of verbal feedback to students individually, or in groups. Some students can be embarrassed when they receive feedback (either positive or critical) in a group situation. It is probably safer to use group situations for more general feedback (for example, discussing common misconceptions or errors), and to save highly specific feedback for one-to-one feedback opportunities.

7   **Prepare *your* script.** When you have a lot of verbal feedback to give to a group of students, it is useful to make notes in advance, to save you having to remember on the spot the particular feedback messages you intend to give to each student. It is sometimes useful to prepare these notes in a form that allows students to take them away from the feedback exchange, serving them as an *aide-mémoire* when they reflect further on the feedback.

8   **Help students to get feedback at the right times.** It can be frustrating for students if they are eager to talk to you to gain some detailed feedback, but keep coming to seek you when you're elsewhere. It can be useful to pin a sheet of paper to your door, listing two or three slots when you know you will be available and asking students to 'book themselves an appointment' by writing their names on the sheet, and the time when they intend to come to see you. This also allows them the chance to think ahead to exactly what they may want to ask you when they talk with you.

9   **Sometimes face-to-face feedback is necessarily going to be hard on students.** At such times it's tempting to use other means of giving feedback – written, printed, email, and so on. However, sometimes it is important that you are there in person so you can explain, and offer support and comfort. When you know this will be the case, try to find something positive to tell them about their work, particularly at the beginning of the interview – and maybe also at the very end.

10 **Respond to what you see in their faces as you proceed.** One of the main advantages of giving feedback verbally is that you can estimate the effect it is having (which is much harder to do with written feedback). You can monitor students' facial expressions, and if they seem to be over-sensitive to critical comment you have the opportunity to soften your approach accordingly.

40

Helping students into peer assessment

Peer assessment allows students to gain a great deal more feedback than they could gain just from their tutors. Moreover, the acts of working out assessment criteria and using them to measure each other's performance help deepen students' understanding of the work they assess. The following suggestions may help you maximise the benefits your students can derive from engaging in peer assessment.

1   **Take care not to impose peer assessment on your students against their will.** Accept that there will be at least some students who regard it as your duty to do the assessing yourself. They may even argue, 'You're paid to assess my work – why should I assess anyone else's work?' It is therefore necessary to spend some time helping them to appreciate that there are very powerful benefits they can gain from peer assessment – particularly those resulting from deeper learning experience.

2   **Help students to see what's in it for them.** Show students how useful it is for them to become more familiar with assessment criteria, increasing their ability to prepare themselves for formal assessments such as exams. Peer assessment is a good way of helping them understand not only how assessment criteria are formulated, but also how they are applied in practice.

3   **Choose with care the task that is to be peer-assessed.** Try to find something where it will be particularly advantageous for students to get feedback from each other, and where a high level of specific expertise is not necessary to apply assessment criteria. Presentations, essays, reports, dissertations, posters and displays all lend themselves to peer assessment if the conditions are appropriate.

4   **Take time getting the criteria right.** The most important factors that determine the success (or otherwise) of peer assessment are the clarity and objectivity of the assessment criteria. 'Interesting', 'stimulating', 'coherent' and 'well structured' are terms that require additional descriptive detail if they

are to be clear enough in everyone's mind to be used objectively as parts of peer assessment criteria.

5   **Do a risk assessment.** Where possible, minimise the feeling of risk that students may feel regarding being measured by each other. For example, if the final scores count for only a small fraction of the coursework total, the feeling of risk is reduced. Alternatively, it could be agreed that the peer assessment will be done purely as a learning experience (i.e. scores will not count) – though then students may not engage in it so seriously.

6   **Develop student ownership of the criteria where possible.** For example, allow the students themselves to generate the assessment criteria and agree as a group on the weighting of each criterion (as well as agreeing on what each criterion actually will mean in practice). When students have a sense of ownership of the criteria, they apply them more diligently than when they use other people's criteria.

7   **Ensure that there are not too many criteria.** For example, students peer-assessing each other's presentations can do so very well when using half a dozen criteria, but it would become much too complex if they tried to use 20 criteria simultaneously. It is better, in peer assessment, to have a few criteria working well than a lot working badly.

8   **Help students to make their peer assessment decisions quickly and easily.** It helps to prepare a grid with a list of the agreed criteria down the left-hand side, a column showing the score given to each criterion, and columns for students to enter their mark for each successive piece of work being assessed. After all the assessments have been completed, the grids can be collected in, averages computed and rank orders decided.

9   **Consider turning the criteria into checklist questions.** It can be best if the questions are relatively short and sharp, and, where it would be relatively straightforward, to divide the available marks for that question. Or agree a scale with the students. For example, 'How good was the content?', worth 10 marks altogether in the example grid (Figure 1), could be scaled '10 = absolutely excellent', '7 = good', '5 = adequate', '3 = poor', '1 = terrible!'.

10 **Make the process more important than the product.** Help students to appreciate that while the averaged results will give them useful information, it is unproductive to challenge particular low or high scores in a personal way. If the group of students is very robust, however, it can be interesting to ask members of the group to justify their decision to award particularly high or low scores.

Presentation			A	B	C	D	E	F	G
Criteria checklist		Weight							
1	How good was the introduction?	6							
2	How good was the content?	10							
3	How strong was the conclusion?	7							
4	How well did it keep to time?	5							
5	How much evidence of research was there?	8							
6	How well were the slides produced and used?	6							
7	How confidently were questions handled?	10							
8	How enthusiastic was the presenter?	8							
Total		60							

Figure 1 An example of a peer assessment grid that could be used by students assessing seven presentations (A–G), where each presentation is marked out of a total of 60, using eight criteria in the form of checklist questions weighted as shown. Similar grids can be designed for peer-assessing essays, reports, artefacts, and so on.

11 **Make the most of the quantity of feedback that peer assessment can deliver.** Students can get much more feedback from a group of their peers than they would have been able to get from one expert witness – the tutor. Having the tutor act as an ordinary member of the group, giving scores in the same way as everyone else, combines the benefits of abundant feedback and authoritative feedback.

41

Helping students into self-assessment

It has been said that anyone who needs an assessor is not adequately prepared to go out into the 'real world'. Self-assessment is a useful transferable skill, and can be cultivated by using it as an integral part of programmes.

1   **Get students reflecting.** Help students to see the usefulness of measuring their own work as a way of looking more deeply at things they have done, and enhancing their understanding of subjects and concepts. Advise students that the most important aspects of self-assessment are not the actual grades or scores that students may award themselves. Much more important are the opportunities to reflect on work they have done, and the chance to think about the nature of assessment criteria related to the work.

3   **Don't worry that students will just give themselves high marks.** It is easy to dismiss the use of self-assessment because of suspicions that students 'will be kind to themselves' and will rate their own work over-generously. While it is true that *some* students may do this, it is usual for students on average to be rather harder when self-assessing their work than tutors would be.

4   **Foster student ownership of the criteria.** It is useful to help students to generate the criteria that they subsequently employ during self-assessment. The greater the feeling of ownership students have over such criteria, the more objectively they will apply them.

5   **Start from 'features of a good [whatever it is]'.** A useful way of generating criteria to be used in self-assessment is to ask each student to write down, for example, 'features of a successful report'. Then get students into groups of three or four and ask each group to shortlist the four most important features. Ask the groups then to turn each 'feature' into a checklist question that would determine whether the feature had been adequately demonstrated (i.e. into assessment criteria). Ask each group for its most important checklist

question and compile a list of a dozen or so such criteria. From such a list, discuss and agree on the most useful of the criteria which have emerged.

6   **Self-assessment doesn't have to be an exact science.** Whereas with peer assessment it is necessary for everyone involved to be using the same set of criteria, with self-assessment there is room for manoeuvre. For example, five 'core' criteria could be agreed, which everyone would use in the self-assessment, but a further three 'additional' criteria could be left to each individual to formulate. These 'additional' criteria could then be formulated specially to take into account individual approaches to the task to be self-assessed.

7   **Intervene only when really necessary.** Where assessment marks or scores are to contribute to the formal assessment profile of students, it may be necessary to involve tutors in a 'moderating' role. For example, tutors could themselves assess the pieces of work, and if the respective assessments were significantly different (for example, by more than 5 per cent), negotiations could take place to decide an agreed grade or score. In practice, it is only for about one case in ten that such negotiations prove to be needed.

8   **Save yourself time assessing.** Acting as a moderator in self-assessment processes can be far easier than assessing work 'from scratch'. It is much quicker to 'skim' work, checking whether agreed assessment criteria have been self-applied objectively, than to apply the criteria 'from cold'. Self-assessment can therefore save tutors time – which is particularly important when large numbers of students are involved.

9   **Give students feedback on the process, not just the product.** Probably the most useful contributions tutors can make to self-assessment processes is to give students feedback on *the quality of their self-assessment*. This feedback progressively leads students to more objective self-assessment.

10   **Expect at least some resistance to the idea.** It is to be expected that a small minority of students will regard it as a 'right' to receive tutor assessment, and will object in principle to being asked to self-assess their work. If they remain unconvinced by explanations of how they can benefit from self-assessment, it is best to defer to their wishes and provide such students with traditional tutor assessment. It is important that the group as a whole is not allowed to feel that the use of self-assessment is any kind of abdication from duty on the part of tutors.

Agreed criteria	Weight	Self-assessment score	Student comments	Tutor feedback
1				
2				
3				
4				
5				
Individual criteria				
6				
7				
8				
Total				

Figure 2 An example of a grid which students could use to self-assess their own work against some agreed criteria, with space for students to identify additional criteria with particular relevance to their individual approaches to the task. Students can add comments to support their self-assessment scores, and receive feedback on their self-assessment from their tutor.

42

Starting up self-assessment student dialogues

Where students hand in work for tutor assessment, it can be useful to get them to self-assess their own work at the time of handing it in, using a 'dialogue' starter pro forma such as that illustrated in Figure 3 overleaf. However, there are hundreds of possible questions that could be used to start off such a dialogue, and the example is only intended to alert you to a few of the possibilities. This process can be useful in helping you to decide where students really need some support and advice, as well as providing a quick means for giving them feedback comments on their work.

	Self-assessment question	Student's response	Feedback from tutor
1	What do you think is the grade your work has earned?		
2	Which part of your work do you consider the best in this assignment?		
3	Which part of the assignment did you find most difficult, and why?		
4	What do you think has been the most important thing you learned as a result of doing this assignment?		
5	Which part of the assignment took you most time to complete?		
6	Which sources did you find most useful in your work on this assignment, and why?		
7	What would you now do differently if you were starting this assignment again?		
8	What advice would you give to someone about to start this assignment?		
9	What feedback would you particularly like about your work on this assignment?		
10	Are there any questions you would like me to try to answer about this topic at this stage?		

Figure 3 Example of a self-assessment pro forma

43

Helping students to negotiate learning agreements

A useful way of empowering students, and of giving them a greater sense of ownership of their learning, is to help them to negotiate learning agreements. The following steps can be helpful in such processes.

1   **Help students to take charge of their own learning.** Convince students that it is useful and beneficial for them to have the additional flexibility and control that they gain by negotiating learning agreements. This can also give them a greater degree of choice over the detailed nature of their studies.

2   **Learning agreements can be negotiated in different ways.** For example, a detailed proposal can be drawn up by each student and then used as the basis for a single negotiation with a tutor, the outcome of which is a negotiated agreement. Alternatively, the negotiations can be staged, and successive elements of the agreement progressively approved, such as the intended outcomes, the processes to be used, the timescale and the products.

3   **Encourage students to negotiate with each other too.** While the most significant parts of negotiated learning agreements usually involve tutor–student negotiations, remind students how useful it can be to practise negotiating with each other as a way of preparing themselves for the ways in which they will present their proposals at the real negotiation session.

4   **Think about group negotiations too.** Negotiated learning agreements lend themselves both to agreements between a tutor and each single student, and to agreements between one or more tutors and a group of students. Group agreements may be rather more complex if it is also necessary to assess in some way the respective contributions of each member of the group to the final product the group delivers.

5   **Start with the intended learning outcomes.** Explain to students that the most important starting point for any learning agreement is a clear, detailed

set of learning outcomes, to form the basis for their negotiated agreements. From these outcomes it can be judged in due course whether the level of the work to be completed is appropriate and realistic. The outcomes should also make it clear exactly why the work is being structured in the ways chosen.

6 **Having decided 'what?', move on to 'how?'.** Having worked out a set of intended outcomes, the logical next step is to summarise the processes that will be used to achieve each of the outcomes. Encourage students to think of more than one way each outcome could be achieved, so that in the process of negotiating the learning agreement it can be decided which approaches are the most recommendable ones.

7 **Then move on to the evidence.** Having sorted out the outcomes and processes, help students to work out how best in due course they can demonstrate their achievement of the outcomes. Get students to work out which forms of evidence (for example, reports, presentations, case studies), most closely relate to demonstrating that the outcomes will have been achieved successfully. When negotiating a range of agreements with a large group of students, it becomes necessary for tutors to give some guidance on the format the product should take (otherwise some students may well spend an inordinate amount of time developing products that are highly advanced).

8 **Next, address 'when?'.** When the outcomes and the processes have been decided on, the next important decision is to place a timescale on the work involved. Encourage students to set interim deadline proposals for various stages of the work they plan to do, rather than simply setting themselves a final deadline.

9 **Next get students to think about the standards.** Allow them some freedom to work out how high they are aiming, and help them to make realistic decisions on this. It is useful to use the negotiation session to devise assessment criteria for the products of the work. These criteria can normally be closely related to the intended outcomes underpinning the work.

10 **Don't be too rigid.** It can be useful to negotiate in a certain amount of flexibility. For example, an agreement can incorporate processes for an accepted amount of renegotiation for circumstances in which it becomes clear while carrying out the agreed work that additional or different aspects should be investigated further.

44

Helping students to revise productively

If students worked steadily throughout their studies, there would be no need for the more concentrated work known as revision, cramming or swotting. However, it would appear that human nature dictates that the need for revision is inevitable. Left to themselves, students often adopt revision techniques that are far from productive. Exams measure the quality of revision much more than the quantity of revision. The following suggestions can help students focus their energies effectively.

1   **It's never too early to start!** As soon as students have something to revise, it's possible to start. Point out how much more enjoyable – and efficient – revision is when there is no threatening exam looming up.

2   **Get students to give you their best reasons for not having started revising yet.** Then talk them through the fact that most of the reasons they come up with are excuses rather than reasons. Point out that they are in fact 'RATs' – revision avoidance tactics. Once they are aware of them, they're less likely to bite!

3   **Take away the fear of the unknown.** Remind students that it is in fact very useful indeed to find something they don't know yet. That means there is time to get to know it. Every question that they can't yet answer is no longer an unknown quantity, but something that can be worked on.

4   **Help students to have tools to use for revision.** For example, provide students with lots of questions to practise with. Exams measure primarily students' ability to answer questions, so such practice is one of the most relevant activities students can engage in when preparing for exams.

5   **Get students to formulate lists of questions for themselves, to practise with.** Some help regarding what sort of question is useful may be required. Questions that students have formulated themselves are owned by the

students, and their efforts to become able to answer such questions are enhanced considerably.

6   **Show students exactly how their exam papers will be structured.** When students know what kinds of questions to expect, they can focus their preparations to answer them. Give students the chance to apply assessment criteria to their own (and each other's) work. The act of assessing helps them remember criteria of the sort they need in due course to live up to.

7   **Help students to be creative and realistic about how they prefer to revise.** Help them to make their own range of revision aids for each of the ways they like to learn – for example, posters for visual learning, audio tapes for students who find they learn a lot by listening, summary and quiz cards for students who like to keep their learning active, and collaborative team programmes for students who like learning alongside other people.

8   **Encourage students to quiz each other.** This can be more productive (and less intimidating) than working on their own. It gives them the chance to practise answering questions 'on the spot' at random, rather than from their own lists. It also allows students the opportunity to learn by explaining things to each other.

9   **Alert students to the dangers of passive reading.** Remind them how easy it is to read something time and time again, but still not become able to apply it. Revision should be considered productive only if some writing activity is in progress, or when practising answering questions in one way or another.

10 **Encourage students to make really concise summaries of information.** The act of summarising helps them prioritise their subject matter, and a collection of good summaries helps reduce the task of revision to manageable proportions.

11 **Suggest that students revise in frequent short spells** rather than long continuous ones. Concentration spans last minutes rather than hours! There's no point sitting for hours on end if no learning pay-off is accruing.

12 **Encourage students to bring variety to their revision.** Frequent changes of subject matter increase learning pay-off. Sticking with each topic for no more than half an hour at a time is a useful ground rule. A change is as good as a rest – and much more productive.

13 **Help students to know when to stop revising.** Exams can be highly stressful and can trigger mental health problems. Help students to distinguish between what comprises reasonable and unreasonable study schedules.

45

Helping students to pass exams

Whatever exams are intended to measure, the one certainty is that they measure students' abilities to answer exam questions. The suggestions below outline some ways of developing students' abilities to answer exam questions logically, quickly and successfully.

1   **Help students gain familiarity with the appearance and structure of exam papers.** In this context, familiarity breeds confidence. When students are used to the appearance of exam papers, there is less chance that they will react in a tense, disorganised manner in their exams. Let them see examples of exam questions very early in their programme, so they know what to expect in due course regarding the general standards they should aim to meet.

2   **Allow students to apply assessment criteria to good – and bad – examples of candidates' answers.** Students are quick to learn exactly where marks can be lost – or gained. A lecture slot getting students to apply the marking scheme that was actually used in a past exam can teach them a great deal about the topic concerned, and provide some useful learning about exams in general.

3   **Emphasise the importance of good timekeeping in exams.** Point out the logic that if students attempt (for example) only two-thirds of the paper, their maximum score is only 66 per cent. Exams measure time management as well as knowledge. Suggest that students should divide their time according to the available marks, having first subtracted 15 or 20 minutes to use at the end of the exam to edit and improve their answers.

4   **Give students practice at interpreting exam questions.** Ask them to decide exactly what each question requires – and what it does not require. Help students identify the key words in exam questions, notably 'why?', 'how?', 'what?', 'when?', 'compare', 'discuss', 'explain', 'give an example of',

and so on. Illustrate to them what each of these question-words is likely to require, in the context of their own subject matter.

5   **Help students become more skilled at choosing which questions to attempt.** When students have a choice of questions, point out how important it is for them not to waste time and energy on what turns out to be a 'bad question' for them – that just leads to depression and panic. The best way to make sensible choices is to read each question in turn slowly, calmly – and more than once. Only then is it possible to make an informed choice regarding which questions to attempt.

6   **Encourage students to re-read each question several times while answering it.** Point out that more marks are lost in exams by students 'going off at tangents' than through any other single cause. Frequent re-reading of the questions can prevent tangents altogether. Suggest that every five minutes or so they look again at the question and ask themselves, 'am I still answering the question?'

7   **Highlight the importance of showing how an answer has been derived.** Stress the value in quantitative questions of showing examiners exactly how an answer has been reached. If examiners can see exactly where an error occurred, they can give due credit for all the parts of the answer that were correctly attempted. Conversely, if examiners can only see the 'wrong' answer, they can't give any marks at all.

8   **Help students to spare themselves from mental blanks.** When students get stuck because something won't come back to mind, encourage them to move to some other question they can answer well. Leaving a gap and moving on is better than sitting getting into a panic. What matters is scoring points on the whole paper, not getting a particular question absolutely right.

9   **Remind students that examiners are human.** Examiners *like* to be able to award marks – they are not simply searching for mistakes! Examiners respond best to clear, well-laid-out answers.

10   **Get students to allow time for editing their answers.** Point out the benefits of saving some time towards the end of each exam for a complete re-reading of the script. Students can pick up many extra marks as they re-read, by correcting obvious errors and adding important further details that will have surfaced in their minds since they wrote their answers.

46

What do exams really measure? A discussion checklist

The questions below may be useful for you to use as a discussion agenda with your students, as you help them to prepare for what will be measured by 'traditional' exams – time-constrained (against the clock), and 'unseen' (don't know what the questions are until sitting in the exam room).

Twenty-one factors measured by time-constrained unseen written exams
1 How much you know about your subject
2 How much you *don't* know about your subject
3 The *quantity* of revision that you have done
4 The *quality* of revision that you have done
5 How intelligent you are
6 How much work you've done the night before
7 How well you keep your cool

8 How good your memory is	
9 How good you are at question-spotting	
10 How fast you think	
11 How fast you write	
12 How legible your handwriting is	
13 How good you are at answering exam questions	
14 How carefully you read the questions	
15 How wisely you choose the questions that you attempt	
16 How well you manage your time during exams	
17 How well you keep exactly to the questions in your answers	
18 How well you set out your answers to the questions	
19 How skilled you are at solving problems	
20 How carefully you read your answers after writing them	
21 How well you edit and improve your answers after reading them	

47

Helping students to get ready for vivas

In some programmes, everyone has vivas (spoken question-and-answer exams or tests). In other programmes, vivas may be used only at the end, mainly to work out what to do with borderline cases. As with other aspects of study skills, it can pay dividends to help students to prepare constructively for vivas.

1   **Make the role of vivas clear to students.** If vivas are used as a normal part of your programme, explain exactly how much they will count for, and when they will take place.

2   **Try to take away any fear of vivas.** Where vivas are used to help decide what to do with borderline cases, explain that normally a viva means a chance to move 'up' rather than to move 'down'. Emphasise also that it is then normal to include representative candidates from 'mid-range' to provide a frame of reference (and that such candidates should certainly not be apprehensive about the fact that they are having a viva).

3   **Take into account students' feelings about vivas.** Accept that some students have an instinctive fear of the public sort of scrutiny they may feel in the situation of a viva. They quite naturally may feel intimidated at the prospect of being questioned by one or more experts or 'figures of authority'.

4   **Point out the benefits of becoming better at doing well in vivas.** Suggest to students that the skills of doing well in viva situations are worth developing consciously. Similar skills will be needed many times during their careers – for example, at interviews, promotion boards, and so on.

5   **Get students practising.** Confirm that skills at handling viva situations effectively (like most other practical skills) are best developed through practice. Encourage students to set up their own mock viva panels and to practise until they feel quite comfortable in the situation of being 'put on the

spot'. Postgraduate students preparing for PhD vivas often spend many weeks practising in this way together.

6   **Help students to work out how best to prepare.** Advise students that there are particular preparations they can make in advance of a viva. They don't have to simply hope that 'it'll be all right on the day'. For example, they can decide what *won't* be expected of them in a viva – for example, lengthy computations or derivations, and so on.

7   **Encourage students to work out what sort of questions they could be asked.** Remind students that a viva is essentially a question-and-answer session, and most of the questions will be quite short. They can therefore prepare for a viva by working out as many likely questions as they can think of, and practising giving oral answers to them.

8   **Suggest to students that it could be useful for them to think back to what they didn't do well in other assessments.** When a viva is being used as a second-chance process, it will usually be because something has not worked out well in another part of the assessment scheme – for example, a poorer-than-expected exam performance. It is then quite likely that part of the viva will focus on the exam that went wrong. It is therefore useful to advise students to check up on things that they know may have gone wrong in their exams as part of their preparations for a viva.

9   **Help students to be aware of the need to create a favourable impression.** It can be useful to show a group of students preparing for vivas some video clips of different behaviours shown by candidates (preferably role-played). Better still, if all the students are preparing for a similar viva, let them capture some of their role-playing on video, then watch themselves.

10 **Caution students about the dangers of 'waffling'!** Unkind examiners in vivas have been known to allow students to dig themselves in deeper and deeper once they have started to invent answers to questions. As with interviews, it is usually much safer to come clean when one simply does not know the answer to a question – after having had the question clarified if necessary.

Chapter 6

Skills for career and life in general

In this final chapter we give some general suggestions covering some of the skills students will need throughout their careers, and particularly some of the skills they will need when looking for employment.

48

Helping students to cope with being away from home

Even though nowadays many students study at home, and a high proportion of students are mature in age, many still leave the family nest for the first time to live away to study. That first experience of taking full responsibility for life away from home is probably even more important to many students than the content of their studies. Perhaps this is where their *education* begins (not just their training). The following suggestions may help you help them.

1 **Accept that a lot may be going on in their lives at this point.** Accept that for many students, being away from home for the first extended time is a cause of both stress and excitement. Acknowledge that at times their full attention will not be on their studies in general, or on your subject in particular.

2 **Get students to think about it and talk to each other about it.** In a lecture or tutorial, near the start of the programme give some time to a group task in which students list both the benefits of the experience of living away from home, and the drawbacks associated with being away from home.

3 **Help students to build on their strengths.** Ask students to work out the positive learning experiences that can be drawn from adapting to living away from home, and explore how these learning experiences can transfer productively to later developments in their education and careers.

4 **Encourage students to form self-help groups.** It can be really useful for them to identify some like-minded classmates and gain from each other mutual support and advice regarding any problems they encounter because of the changes they are experiencing in their lives at this stage in their education.

5 **Help them to find some role models.** Suggest that groups of students invite some final-year students as expert witnesses, to share ways and means that they used to adapt to living away from home.

6   **Encourage students to find a mentor, and also to be mentors to each other.** Help them to work out role descriptions for mentors, and to address the benefits that can be gained by mentors as well as by those being mentored.

7   **Help students to keep in contact with those back at home.** One problem of being away from home is the danger of losing friends by failing to keep in contact. Suggest that a very short email or note is often enough to keep channels of communication open.

8   **Don't wait till things have 'settled down'!** Point out the danger of putting off corresponding with (or telephoning) contacts at home. In fast-moving experiences of higher education, things are unlikely ever to 'settle down'. Meanwhile, friends and relatives at home can become anxious and difficult.

9   **Encourage students to tune in to their new locations.** Do what you can to help students to develop new roots in their new environment. It can be useful to start a seminar or tutorial now and then with an icebreaker round such as 'What's the best thing about this town that you discovered last week – and the worst thing?'

10 **Remind students about existing channels of help.** Explain how valuable people such as counsellors, advisers and personal tutors can be when needed – but that they can't help unless their help is sought. Encourage students to seek out such people even when they have no particular worries, simply to get to know them. Remind them, for example, that for someone like a counsellor, a meeting with a student *without* a problem is a pleasant change!

49

Helping students to cope with stress

Few people have not had to cope with stress at one time or another. Many people seem to cope with long-term continual stress. Stress can be felt more deeply by people who are coping with it for what seems to them like 'the first time' – this includes many students in higher education.

1   **Help students to accept that stress is a natural part of life.** It does not help at all simply to rail at the situation or allocate blame. There's no shame in feeling stressed now and then. It's just normal.

2   **Help students to turn stress into opportunity.** Convince students that every stressful situation can be viewed as a useful learning experience. Coping with stress – even temporarily 'going under' as a result of stress – can be used to build up coping strategies.

3   **Help students decide when they are really stressed rather than a little harassed.** Point out that a person who is clinically stressed may not realise this. It often takes other people to see that someone is overstressed. Encourage students to talk to each other about how they feel, and to be willing to advise each other when symptoms of excessive stress are evident.

4   **Remind students that a certain amount of stress is actually healthy.** Adrenalin levels can be raised a little, and performance can be improved. The only sort of stress to worry about is when stress gets in the way of a balanced and enjoyable life, or when it starts to have repercussions on other people.

5   **Point out that help is all around students.** Encourage students who feel they may be stressed to use any or all of the avenues of help open to them. Counsellors, chaplains, programme tutors, doctors, advisers, neighbours and fellow students can all provide tangible help to people who are overstressed.

6 **Go on a course about it?** Sometimes the best time to address the topic of stress is when one is completely unstressed. It can therefore be quite useful to attend a session on stress management without any particular reason for attending, simply as a learning experience to store for later use if needed.

7 **Get students to adopt each other's coping tactics.** Encourage students to exchange their own experiences at coping with stressful situations. Many find particular hobbies or relaxation techniques serve them well, and can introduce the techniques to others.

8 **'Don't resort to blaming people.'** Other people are often blamed for causing stress. In fact, there is little anyone can do to alter how other people behave. It is usually much more productive to consider altering how one reacts to other people's behaviour. Therefore, advising students to retain ownership of how they react to stressful situations is more useful than trying to find ways of changing each situation for them.

9 **Many kinds of stress are avoidable.** For example, the stress many students feel during intensive revision can be avoided by planning the revision well, starting it early and doing it less intensively. Suggest to students ways in which they can identify future stress situations in advance, and act early to minimise the stresses.

10 **Encourage students not to hide from failure.** One of the biggest stress factors in the very back of many students' minds is the threat of the possibility of failure. Suggest that they allow themselves to think about it, and therefore take actions to minimise the possibility of it. Encourage students likely to be *overstressed* about possible failure to regard failure as simply a temporary – if inconvenient – setback, and an experience that itself provides useful learning experiences.

50

Helping students to recover from two weeks off!

Most students will, at some point in their studies, need to take time off, owing to circumstances quite beyond their control (illness, bereavement in the family, personal problems, and so on). With large groups, it can be difficult for tutors to know when help is needed, and how to provide such help. The following suggestions may assist.

1   **Keep yourself informed.** Create mechanisms whereby students who need to take time off alert you to the fact. Checking up who misses tutorials can be one way of finding out who may have a problem. Keep records so that you find out (and can offer to help) before any student may have dropped out for too long.

2   **Get students to help you find out who may need help.** Create a climate where students who know of fellow students with problems feel that they can alert their tutors to the situation. When it is clear that you're not simply being dogmatic about attendance at lectures and seminars, students are usually willing to alert you to any real difficulties they know their colleagues are facing.

3   **Keep back-up materials to help anyone who can't be present at any important session.** Build up a collection of resources you can give out to students who have missed vital classes. Copies of your own lecture notes may be useful. Questions, problems and case studies that were dealt with in the missed sessions are likely to be particularly useful. References to textbooks that would cover the missed sessions will also be useful.

4   **Help students who are trying to catch up.** For students who have necessarily missed part of their studies, it is particularly important that they feel they can ask questions about anything they can't understand as they try to get back on track. Give the students concerned a definite time and place to approach you with any problems they have.

5   **Encourage students to help each other.** Explain to the whole group that it is a very useful learning experience to explain something one has just learned. The act of putting it into words to explain it to a fellow human being is a good way of understanding it oneself.

6   **Help students realise that it's best not to spend so much time catching up that they miss out on what's going on here and now.** Otherwise they will tend to continue to remain behind, and that dampens morale. Suggest they catch up 'a bit at a time' while continuing with the work being done in class at present.

7   **Be flexible where possible about deadlines.** Where students have necessarily missed deadlines for coursework, it may be worth coming to 'special arrangements' – for example, setting a deadline for a rough outline of the work to be submitted, with a later deadline for the final submission. This can allow you to be alerted to any significant problems that may have been caused by the time out. It is also better than allowing them to miss out altogether on the element of coursework concerned, with adverse effects cumulatively at the end of the programme or module.

8   **Minimise the occurrence of 'must do' elements.** Where possible, build in choices and alternatives, particularly regarding coursework (and also exam questions). When students have such choices, it becomes less critical that they catch up on absolutely everything they may have missed.

9   **Try to provide alternative pathways.** There is never just one way of learning something. Especially for students who miss things through no fault of their own, try to have other ways in which they can make up for lost time, or alternative things they can do to compensate for missed deadlines.

10 **Help students who have missed something to keep a sensible perspective.** One small point that is not 'understood' can seem like a mountain, when in fact it may not be significant at all. Remind students that any problem is only a problem till they find out how to solve it.

51

Helping students to recover from failure

There are few people who haven't experienced failure at some points in their lives. Yet students who have failed often feel that it's entirely their own fault, and that they should not expect any help from their tutors. However, there is much that tutors can do to help students recover from failure. The following suggestions may help you to help those students who, for one reason or another, don't manage to succeed first time on your programmes.

1   **Help students not to hide from failure.** When students have failed at something, help them to accept it. Running away from it may be an instinctive reaction, but it does not help them to prevent a similar thing happening in the future. Once students have accepted that a particular episode was unsuccessful, they can begin structured preparations to guarantee that it will be successful next time.

2   **Help students to turn failure to their advantage.** Help students suffering from depression after failure, to look at it as a learning opportunity. Point out how unimportant and fruitless it is for them to dwell on 'letting people down' feelings. Remind them that every successful person has recovered from failures at one time or another. Advise them to work out constructively exactly what they were not able to do on that particular occasion.

3   **Tell students to avoid thoughts that begin with 'if only . . . '.** Such thoughts tend to be unproductive. They don't solve things. Whatever the situation, suggest that students should live with the art of the possible, and think creatively about what they can do about the failure.

4   **'When you're in a hole, stop digging!'** Advise students that in their earnest endeavours to get out of the hole, they should not 'go and make it even deeper'. Now is the time to do something else. Find something useful to do that's not too hard.

5   **Emphasise that having failed at something does not mean that one *is* a failure.** Explain that 'failure' is a transient stage, when what the students managed to do simply did not yet match what they were required to do at that stage. Having failed does not mean that they 'can't ever do it'; it simply meant they 'couldn't yet do it' that time round.

6   **Explain that it is really useful to keep up to date with what one can't yet do.** Remind students how valuable it is to pinpoint exactly what they can't yet do. Only when they have this knowledge can they systematically fine-tune their learning to eliminate the possibility of the same thing going wrong in the future.

7   **Celebrate learning through mistakes.** Give examples of how getting something wrong is one of the most effective ways of eventually getting it right. Knowing what can cause problems is useful knowledge for the future. In life in general, probably more is learned by getting it wrong at first than by getting it right first time.

8   **Encourage students to learn from each other's experiences of failure.** Suggest that small groups of students who have failed at something can work together to find ways of analysing what caused the failure. Sharing problems with other students in the same situation can be comforting.

9   **Get students to think about the processes that may have let them down.** Where students need to prepare for a resit examination, encourage them to look not only at which parts of the subject caused them difficulties, but at their approaches to learning the subject. It often pays dividends to analyse study skills such as revision and exam technique in the light of an unsuccessful episode.

10 **Sometimes a setback can be a blessing in disguise.** Advise students working for resit examinations that they may indeed find themselves at an advantage in the next stage of their studies. Other students who did not need resits may have forgotten much of their previous knowledge when they return for the next part of their studies, while those who have done resits have it fresher in their minds (and maybe also have a deeper understanding, because of the extra time they have spent studying, and the analysis of past difficulties).

52

Helping students to apply for jobs

Writing an effective CV is one part of making a good application for a job. Other important aspects include writing a suitable letter of application, and (not least) filling in application forms themselves. Giving students practice to help them develop these skills is a useful addition to other parts of their education where you may be able to give them useful support.

1   **Show students how it may be done – and how not to do it, too.** Make a collection of good, bad and indifferent letters of application for posts, and issue these to students as a basis for discussion.

2   **Ask students what they think counts.** Get students themselves to work out criteria for a good letter of application, using your assorted materials to identify strengths and weaknesses exemplified in them.

3   **Give your students something to apply for.** Ask students themselves to draft letters of application for a fictitious post, experimenting with different approaches to the task. If possible, form a 'selection panel' of colleagues (or students from another group) and ask the panel to select what it considers are the best letters, identifying the features that caused these letters to be preferred.

4   **Get them to make their letters of application look good.** Where students need to become acquainted with word-processing systems, help them develop templates of 'letter skeletons' that can be used later to produce specific letters rapidly, by inserting the particular data relating to the post being applied for, and specific comments to support the applications.

5   **Start them practising filling in pro formas.** Collect a range of the sorts of application forms that students may expect to meet from firms and organisations. It can be useful to make overhead transparencies or slides of typical forms, to use in illustrating the sorts of information students will need to have to hand when dealing with such forms.

6 **There's no second chance to make that good first impression.** Remind students of the importance of the appearance of submitted application forms. As it is not easily possible to use word-processing systems to deal with complex forms unless they're supplied electronically, greater care may need to be taken in inputting information onto the forms. Remind students that if their own keyboard skills are underdeveloped, it may be worth their choosing to pay a skilled typist to prepare submission copies of the most important application forms.

7 **Sometimes it pays to copy!** Suggest to students that however many applications they have in the pipeline, it's worth their retaining a photocopy of each form they submit. Those application forms that lead to shortlisting will probably contain much of the information upon which interview questions will be based, so it becomes very useful to refer to the details put into the forms when shortlisted and preparing for interview. Obviously, there's no way of telling *which* forms will get them onto those shortlists, so it's useful to keep copies of *all* serious applications.

8 **Help students to sell themselves well.** Many application forms ask for quite 'deep' answers to quite subtle questions. For example, they may have space for applicants to outline their career aims and ambitions. It is useful to give students some practice at expressing these in a convincing and effective way.

9 **All experience counts.** Remind students that even if they have not yet held any full-time employment posts, it may be well worth their giving details of vacation jobs they have done, particularly when the jobs involved positions of responsibility or trust. To a prospective employer, *any* employment experience is seen as better than none – for example, it's taken as proof that the applicant has already mastered the challenge of getting out of bed and turning up for work on time!

10 **People-skills matter.** Encourage students to use opportunities for their application forms to paint attractive pictures of them as sociable human beings. Employers are unlikely to wish to recruit 'loners' – however gifted academically. For example, leisure activities and hobbies can be a way of demonstrating that applicants are capable of getting on with other people – for example, in societies, clubs, and so on.

53

Helping students to put together their CVs

Apart from obtaining degrees or diplomas successfully, preparing a good curriculum vitae is one of the most important activities that students may do during a college programme. You've doubtless done this yourself several times to be a tutor already. There are many ways that you may be able to assist your students in this process, including those listed below.

1   **Help your students to see that it's an important investment in their future.** Helping them to regard keeping their CVs up to date as important from an early stage is a good idea. Build CV preparation into personal development planning from an early stage in students' studies. Remind them that their skills of written communication (and indeed layout and presentation) are important in helping them to get themselves shortlisted in job applications when they finish their studies.

2   **Let them see how to do it – and how not to do it.** Show them a range of good and not so good examples of CVs. Ask them to make judgements based both on their first impressions of each CV, and on more penetrating analysis.

3   **Help students to work out what to include.** Help them to decide on the main sections to include in an effective CV. For example, give them advice on the balance to be struck between sections such as 'general information', 'education and training', 'employment', 'career aims', 'leisure interests', and so on.

4   **Get them to get other pairs of eyes onto their draft CVs.** All feedback on CVs is useful – even the feedback they may decide to disregard. Ensure that somewhere in their programme of coursework, students have the opportunity not only to prepare a CV, but to receive detailed feedback on its effectiveness from other people, including fellow students, yourself, and anyone who may be persuaded to role-play an employer to help students gain skills at putting their best foot forward in their CVs.

5 **Point out that it's best to be production manager as well as content editor.** Preparing a CV can be coupled with word-processing development. A useful end product gives students a genuine reason for increasing their skills at using word-processing or desktop publishing software. They may well have a need later for the skills they develop – for example when writing project reports or dissertations.

6 **Make it clear what a CV is for.** Help students to identify the aims they should have in mind when putting together their CVs. For example, they should try to pave the way towards interview questions that they will answer with confidence (perhaps on leisure interests), and they should try to find ways of making their achievements and qualifications look impressive and convincing.

7 **Help your students to sell themselves.** Remind them that their CVs need to serve as 'ambassadors' for them, giving an impression of a well-organised, highly motivated and interesting person. Therefore, the structure of the pages and the style and presentation all have roles to play in getting them shortlisted for interview.

8 **Put CVs to the test.** When it is possible to devote sufficient time to CV development, get students to produce the best CV they can, and then constitute a 'real' selection panel (perhaps from another group of students – or better still, use the expertise of any real employer who may be willing to donate some time to help to develop your students' skills) to pick out a shortlist (and to give reasons explaining why selections were made, and why other examples were not chosen).

9 **Help students to help each other become more employable.** Give students encouragement to 'polish' their CVs collaboratively. The detailed feedback they can give each other while editing and refining their CVs can be very valuable. Try to overcome worries about the possibility that they will end up competing directly with each other for exactly the same posts at the end of their studies – statistically this is not nearly as likely as they may think.

10 **Continue to be there for your students.** When the time comes for students to produce their CVs 'for real', they will appreciate continued advice from you. They may in any case wish you to be a referee for their applications, and the more you already know about their CVs, the simpler your task of providing a focused reference may be.

54

Helping students to develop their interview skills

In the final analysis, however successful students are academically, to secure an appointment they need to convince one or more people, face to face, that they're ideal for the post concerned. Interview skills (like most skills) can be learned by trial and error. However, there is much that tutors can do to minimise the 'error'.

1 **Link interview preparation into personal development planning.** Make it part of your programme if time and space are available.

2 **Help students to realise how important interpersonal skills actually are.** Although they are not directly assessed in most higher education programmes, students still need them to move on from college. Establish the importance of face-to-face communication skills in life in general. Remind students that if other people are to be convinced by them, they often have to do the convincing face to face. Getting the job they really want may depend on giving a good interview.

3 **Suggest that all practice will be useful.** Help students to appreciate that face-to-face communication is learned best by practice and trial and error, but that much of the learning can be done in 'safe' situations such as role-play exercises with their peers.

4 **Prepare students for the expected.** Sometimes at interviews, candidates are requested to 'tell us a bit about yourself'. Open-ended questions like this can be harder to deal with than direct questions. Use a tutorial or seminar session to allow each member of the group to give a short (three-minute) description of his or her education and background. The main purposes of this are simply to help students become more comfortable when talking about themselves, and to get students used to the sound of their own voices engaged in this activity.

5   **Prepare them for the tougher questions too.** A trickier interview question is 'Well, then, will you tell us exactly why we should offer *you* the post?' Again, this is something that can be developed by practice. An appropriate balance between modesty and 'blowing one's own trumpet' is required, and the feedback that students can receive from each other (and from you) can be very useful in helping them to develop the right balance.

6   **Let students learn by role-playing.** At an appropriate point in a programme, a little before students are setting out on the main task of job-hunting, it can be worth devoting some time (maybe a few tutorial or seminar slots) to an ongoing role-play scenario as follows. First, get students to produce CVs and application forms (for a fictitious post, for example), and set up interview panels with students role-playing key personnel (training manager, managing director, personnel officer, recruitment manager) for a firm or organisation.

7   **Let them experience all the different parts.** Allow all students to take part in the interviews, once as a candidate and at least once role-playing some of the panel members. Structure the interviews to be as close as possible to real-life scenarios (giving the panel members enough time to read the documentation from each 'candidate' and to prepare questions relevant to the roles they are playing). Have other members of the group as observers, taking notes of 'triumphs' and 'disasters' during the interviews.

8   **Capture what happens.** If possible, use a television studio for some of the interviews, with students operating cameras and editing equipment if possible. It is then possible for candidates to privately view the video of their interviews, learning a great deal from the experience with little need for anyone to talk them through their strengths and weaknesses!

9   **Turn students' experiences into an action planning agenda.** Play back videos of interviews (maybe last year's interviews) to groups of students and use them to generate lists of 'dos and don'ts' for interviews.

10 **Use expert witnesses.** It is often possible to recruit some interested personnel from companies or organisations you have connections with, to constitute some 'real' people for a selection panel. Some firms may even provide a 'prize': a working trip to the United States was provided by one firm we know, for the most successful candidate in some simulated interviews.

11 **Encourage students to practise informally with each other.** Small syndicates can role-play interviews as a regular (and entertaining) part of their social activities, gradually developing members' abilities to be comfortable when put on the spot, and (most important) enhancing the confidence and 'coolness' that will eventually land them the posts they want.

12   **Involve your careers service in helping students to prepare for interviews.** Such services can often offer a great deal of experience and expertise in helping students to prepare for employment, and can supplement the curriculum in a systematic and valuable way.

Some further reading

Allison, B and Race, P (2004) *The Student's Guide to Preparing Dissertations and Theses* London, Routledge.

Barnes, R (1995) *Successful Study for Degrees* London, Routledge.

Beaty, L (July 1997) SEDA Special No 5 *Developing Your Teaching through Reflective Practice* Birmingham, SEDA Publications.

Bell, J (1999) *Doing your Research Project* Buckingham, UK, Open University Press.

Biggs, J (1999) *Teaching for Quality Learning at University* Open University Press/SRHE, Buckingham, UK.

Bligh, D (2000) *What's the Point in Discussion?* Exeter, UK, and Portland, Oregon, Intellect.

Bligh, D (2002) (6th edition) *What's the Use of Lectures?* San Francisco, Jossey-Bass.

Brookfield, SD and Preskill, S (1999) *Discussion as a Way of Teaching* Buckingham, UK, Open University Press.

Brown, G and Atkins, M (1997) *Effective Teaching in Higher Education* London, Routledge.

Brown, S and Glasner, A (eds) (1999) *Assessment Matters in Higher Education: Choosing and Using Diverse Approaches* Buckingham, UK, Open University Press.

Brown, S and Knight P (1994) *Assessing Learners in Higher Education* London, Kogan Page.

Brown, S and Race, P (2002) *Lecturing: A Practical Guide* London, RoutledgeFalmer.

Brown, S, Rust, C and Gibbs, G (1994) *Strategies for Diversifying Assessment in Higher Education* Oxford, Oxford Centre for Staff Development.

Brown, S and Smith, B (ed.) (1996) *Resource-Based Learning* London, Kogan Page (in association with SEDA).

Brown, S and Smith, B (July 1997) SEDA Special No. 3 *Getting to Grips with Assessment* Birmingham, SEDA Publications.

Brown, S and Smith, B (May 1999) SEDA Special No. 8 *Academic Survival Strategies* Birmingham, SEDA Publications.

Chambers, E and Northedge, A (1997) *The Arts Good Study Guide* Milton Keynes, UK, Open University Worldwide.

Cowan, J (1998) *On Becoming an Innovative University Teacher: Reflection in Action* Buckingham, UK, Open University Press.

Creme, P and Lea, MR (2003) (2nd edition) *Writing at University: A Guide for Students* Buckingham, UK, Open University Press.

Cryer, P (2000) *The Research Student's Guide to Success* Buckingham, UK, Open University Press.

Edwards, J, Smith, B and Webb, G (2001) *Lecturing: Case Studies, Experience and Practice* London, RoutledgeFalmer.

Evans, L and Abbott, I (1998) *Teaching and Learning in Higher Education* London, Cassell.

Fairbairn, GJ and Winch, C (1996) (2nd edition) *Reading, Writing and Reasoning: A Guide for Students* Buckingham, UK, Open University Press.

Fry, H, Ketteridge, S and Marshall, S (1999) *A Handbook for Teaching and Learning in Higher Education: Enhancing Academic Practice* Kogan Page, London.

Knight, P (ed.) (1995) *Assessment for Learning in Higher Education* London: Kogan Page (in association with SEDA).

Laurillard, D (1993) *Rethinking University Teaching: A Framework for the Effective Use of Educational Technology* London, Routledge.

Macdonald, R (July 1997) SEDA Special No. 2 *Teaching and Learning in Small Groups* Birmingham, SEDA Publications.

Mortiboys, A (March 2002) SEDA Special No. 12 *The Emotionally Intelligent Lecturer* Birmingham, SEDA Publications.

Northedge, Andy (2004) *The Good Study Guide* Milton Keynes, UK, Open University Worldwide.

Northedge, A, Thomas, J, Lane, A and Peasgood, A (1997) *The Sciences Good Study Guide* Milton Keynes, UK, Open University Worldwide.

O'Hagan, C (July 1997) SEDA Special No. 4 *Using Educational Media to Improve Communication and Learning* Birmingham, SEDA Publications.

Race, Phil (1999) *How to Get a Good Degree* Buckingham, UK, Open University Press.

Race, Phil (ed.) (1999) *2000 Tips for Lecturers* RoutledgeFalmer, London.

Race, Phil (2000) *How to Win as a Final Year Student* Buckingham, UK, Open University Press.

Race, Phil (2003) *How to Study: Practical Tips for Students* Oxford, Blackwell.

Ramsden, P (1992) *Learning to Teach in Higher Education* Routledge, London.

Saunders, Danny (ed.) (1994) *The Complete Student Handbook* Oxford, Blackwell.

Schwartz, P and Webb, G (ed.) (2002) *Assessment: Case Studies, Experience and Practice from Higher Education* London, Kogan Page.

Smith, B (July 1997) SEDA Special No. 1 *Lecturing to Large Groups* Birmingham, SEDA Publications.

Smith, B and Brown, S (ed.) (1995) *Research, Teaching and Learning in Higher Education* London: Kogan Page (in association with SEDA).

Tracy, Eileen (2002) *The Student's Guide to Exam Success* Buckingham, UK, Open University Press.

Index